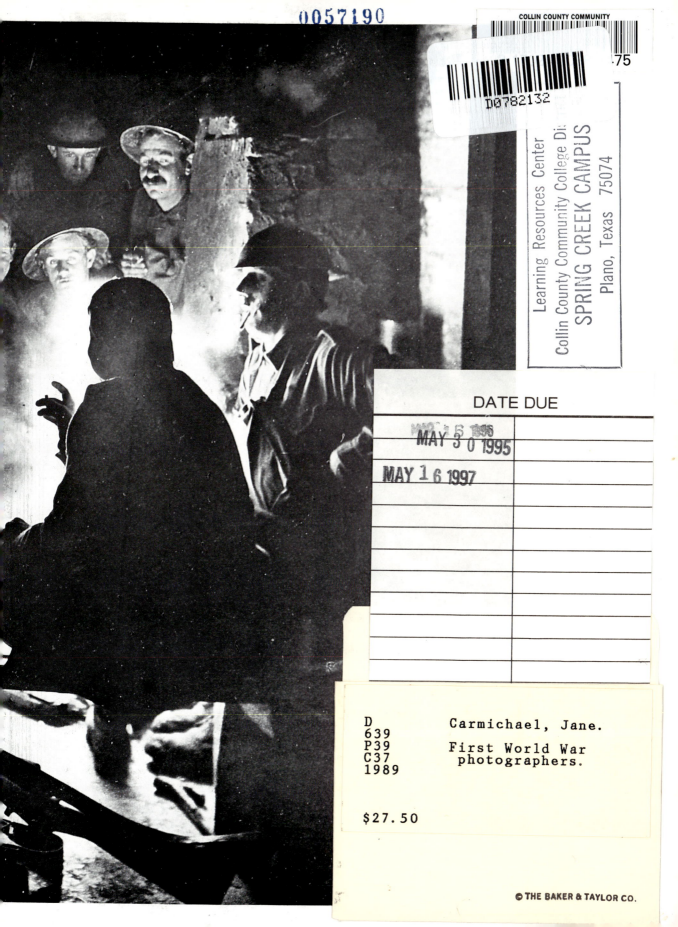

0057190

DATE DUE

MAY 1 6 1995	
MAY 3 0 1995	
MAY 1 6 1997	

FIRST WORLD WAR PHOTOGRAPHERS

Jane Carmichael

Routledge
LONDON AND NEW YORK

First published 1989
by Routledge
11 New Fetter Lane, London EC4P 4EE
29 West 35th Street, New York,
NY 10001

Printed in Great Britain by
Butler & Tanner Ltd
Frome and London

British Library Cataloguing in Publication
Data
First World War photographers
    1. World War 1
    I. Carmichael, Jane
    940.3

ISBN 0 415 01009 8

CONTENTS

FOREWORD

The photographer first went to war in the Crimea, laden with bulky wooden cameras and tripods, boxes of glass plates and bottles of dangerous chemicals; in the early 1850s such encumbrances were the essential tools of a medium barely fifteen years old. Roger Fenton, recognized as a pioneer of war photography, carried all his apparatus in a converted wine merchant's van which became unbearably hot and uncomfortable, moved slowly, and was a perfect target for enemy gunfire. His consciously artistic photographs show nothing of the real action of the campaign; in any case, the wet collodion process of the time was far too slow to capture movement. By technique, circumstance, and temperament, Fenton and his Victorian contemporaries took photographs that were pale shadows of the events they witnessed. Mathew Brady and others in the American Civil War which began five years after the Crimean campaign, perhaps came nearer to revealing some of the horror of war, but nevertheless the most famous of their dramatic photographs had to be posed.

From the 1880s, cameras became progressively smaller and able to take more instantaneous pictures. The development of half-tone printing led to newspapers being illustrated by genuine reproductions and encouraged the profession of press photographer together with the establishment of photographic agencies to sell his work. But, during the First World War, photography and contemporary attitudes towards its publication meant that it was still not ready to keep pace with the action and scale of this enormous conflict. Action reporting in any quantity had to wait for the technical invention of the 35mm camera, introduced in the late 1920s, and the development of the recognized profession of photojournalist, with its elite of courageous war reporters. Robert Capa in Spain in the 1930s and Don McCullin in Vietnam in the 1960s set new standards for committed war reporting.

A study of photographic history might therefore lead one to expect the visual record of the 1914–18 war to be incomplete and unsatisfactory. In fact, however, Jane Carmichael's fascinating exploration of the archives reveals the existence of some 40,000 official photographs more than half of which were taken in the bitter contest of the Western Front. Add to these the pictures taken by press and amateur photographers, and there is a considerable body of historic material from which the illustrations in this book have been selected.

In some ways the amateurs are the most interesting. One of the frequently cited 'stories' of the First World War, the fraternization between the opposing armies on Christmas Day 1914, was in fact recorded by amateurs on their pocket cameras. Many similar photographs found their way to the press in the early part of the war by means of the competitions mounted by the latter to attract material for publication.

The ability of the best still photography to distil the general truth of situations, people, or events is one of its most important characteristics, making it a powerful medium even in the age of film and television. In some ways, the relatively static and formal nature of pre-35mm photography was appropriate to the First World War, the last conflict to be guided by a commanding aristocracy. If we feel sympathy – not to say pity – for the ordinary people in this extraordinary album of war, the formal poses of some of the generals and admirals now seem echoes of a bygone hierarchical and authoritarian age.

Photography can make heroes as well as cut them down to size. Looking at the romanticized portrait of Lawrence of Arabia, one wonders whether he could possibly have become such a legendary figure without the images and film compiled and then so assiduously exploited by Harry Chase and Lowell Thomas.

It is a cliché of photography that 'a picture is worth a thousand words'. But news photography was such an unfamiliar phenomenon in the First World War that the British press actually seemed to prefer words. Sometimes hundreds of words were used by a newspaper to describe what a picture showed, rather than letting it speak for itself. This may have been, at least in part, a reaction to the sheer shortage of pictures. There were only sixteen official British photographers throughout all the theatres of war, compared with double that number for France and three times as many for Germany. The British services maintained their traditional reticence and the Royal Navy in particular found the idea of publishing pictures about its activities hard to accept. Excluded from reporting front-line activities, the professionals turned their attention to the home front, and to the role of civilians in the war effort. Their pictures provide telling evidence of the growing participation of women whose role became more and more vital as the war progressed.

Towards the end of the war, the Imperial War Museum came into being, and actively encouraged the taking of record photographs, as did archives in Australia and Canada. The resulting collections are all too little known, and we owe the present Keeper of the Imperial War Museum's photographic collections, Jane Carmichael, a debt of gratitude for unlocking this priceless source of information. To be reminded of the horrors of war through looking at these and photographs of later conflicts in such repositories is surely a potent way to discourage anyone from ever wanting to go to war again.

Colin Ford
Keeper, National Museum of Photography, Film and Television

ACKNOWLEDGEMENTS

This book is based on one of the nation's great collections, the five million photographs showing the involvement of Britain and her Empire in the two world wars and other conflicts of the twentieth century held by the Imperial War Museum. I am grateful for permission to reproduce my selection here which I hope demonstrates something of the variety and richness of the archive of the First World War. I have also been able to draw on material first published in the *IWM Review* no. 2. Special thanks are due to the staff of the Department of Photographs, especially to the photographer Richard Bayford. The Departments of Printed Books and Documents also provided me with valuable resources.

Very little has been written on the photographers of the First World War and I acknowledge my debt to Dr Stephen Badsey and Dr Nicholas Hiley who both carried out pioneering studies in this field. Peter Robertson of the Public Archives of Canada and Bryan Butler of the Australian War Memorial also supplied much useful information.

I would also like to thank Andrew Wheatcroft of Routledge, Maureen Churchman who drew the maps, and the many friends who egged me on to the finishing line. I should add that drawing generalizations from thousands of photographs is a risky business; my conclusions are entirely my own responsibility about a subject which is complex and arguable.

Jane Carmichael

January 1988

NOTE

Unless otherwise stated, the numbers shown with the photographs are all Imperial War Museum references. Copies may be purchased on application to the Department of Photographs, Imperial War Museum, Lambeth Road, London SE1 6HZ. The archive is open to the public during the week and visitors are welcome.

The Western Front, 1914–18 (*Chapters 2–3*)

NORTH SEA

Zeebrugge
Ostend
Antwerp
Calais
Ghent
Passchendaele
Schelde
Hazebrouck
Ypres
Messines
Brussels
Armentières
BELGIUM
Neuve Chapelle
Montreuil
Loos
Mons
Arras
Cambrai
Sambre
Charleroi
Bapaume
St
Quentin
Le Cateau
Somme
Albert
Amiens

FRANCE

Oise
Soissons
Aisne
Rheims
Seine
Marne
Verdun

Paris

Front line at end of 1914 ― ― ―
Line at end of German
retreat to Hindenburg Line, ∙∙∙∙∙∙∙∙∙∙∙
February 1917
Line on 11 November 1918 ▬▬▬▬

0   20   40 miles

ix

Gallipoli, Palestine, and Mesopotamia, 1914–18 (*Chapters 2 and 4*)

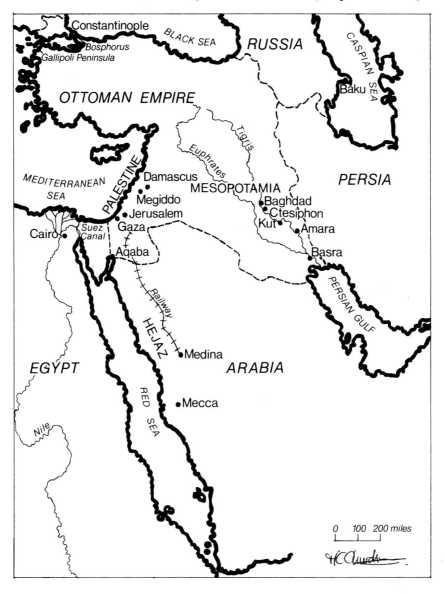

Gallipoli, 1915 (*Chapter 2*)

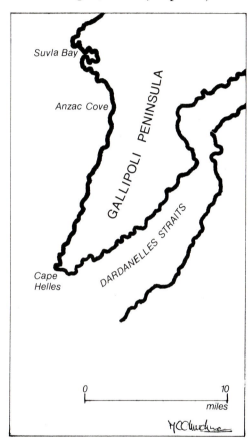

INTRODUCTION

Photographs of the First World War are usually appreciated for what they show, the desolate battlefields of the Western Front, the mighty battleships patrolling the seas, the frail aircraft engaged in a new element of warfare, and the tired soldiers in the trenches. The question of how they came to be taken is seldom asked, yet it is an intriguing episode in photographic history with many participants both professional and amateur. Photographs convey a wealth of visual information in a succinct format and tend to be accepted rather uncritically. However, war photographs in particular are ambivalent documents, which can range from the straightforward record of a scene to those which have been 'helped' towards an appropriate mood or a deliberately contrived misrepresentation. An extra dimension in terms of sensationalism or bias can be added when they are published. By examining the origins and, where appropriate, the publication of some of the photographs taken by British and Imperial photographers during the First World War, considerable insight can be gained into their circumstances, how their work was perceived at the time and how the visual record of war came to be compiled.

During the First World War there were three main categories of photographer; official, press, and amateur. The concept of official war reporting was developed to a greater degree than ever before. Previously, official reporting had usually been done by the forces themselves but now, the much greater extent of the struggle and the growth of the various popular media, meant that the military slowly developed an organization of professionals, appointed specifically for the purpose of compiling material on an authorized and authoritative basis. It was extended to include not only professional war correspondents but photographers, cinematographers and artists. The professional was either integrated completely into the services and given commissioned status or allowed special access on a limited basis. In return for these privileges his work was subject to both military and civilian censorship but was guaranteed a respected status and wide distribution. However, the experiment was limited by military suspicion, political wariness, and the limitations of the professions themselves. The numbers involved in any category remained few. Official photography was no exception but eventually at least one man was appointed to every theatre of war including the civilian and several to the most important battleground, the Western Front. There was much variation in the circumstances of and attitudes towards the appointments both within the services and in the different theatres, which in practice could leave considerable scope for the individual. The work of the official photographers was initially intended for publication in the home press and for circulation as propaganda material abroad but as the struggle continued, their role broadened to include the permanent record for Britain and the Empire.

Ordinary press photographers found themselves severely restricted as they were virtually excluded from the most important battle area, the Western Front. They had a freer hand in some of the peripheral theatres such as Egypt or Mesopotamia and, on occasion, in coverage of the actions of Britain's allies. But as they could not witness the front-line action in the theatre where most of Britain's effort was concentrated, their role was circumscribed. Even at home, dealing with civilian subjects, they could encounter difficulties if they failed to observe stringent regulations regarding permits for photography of military or associated subjects.

Since the turn of the century it had been possible for the serviceman to take a small personal camera to war. During the First World War the amount he could use it depended on where and in which service he was fighting. In some places he might find himself invited by his superior officers to contribute to the press, in others this was highly unlikely. But, given the relatively few official photographers and the restricted role of the press the amateur had an important part to play. He or at times she could record a personal experience of war and on occasion provide unique witness.

The photographs of the First World War offer an extraordinary range of images. With their origins established, they can be appreciated not only for their documentation of one of the great conflicts of the twentieth century but also for the insights they offer into the operations of propaganda and journalism during the period and for the sum of their individual achievements.

1

PHOTOGRAPHIC OPPORTUNITIES:
Controls and techniques 1914–18

By the second decade of the twentieth century war photography had made great strides since its beginnings in the middle of the nineteenth. There were considerable differences in the status, scope, and speed of reproduction of the work of Roger Fenton taking photographs in the Crimean War of 1854–6 and the first and longest serving of the official photographers, Ernest Brooks, covering the battlefields of the Western Front in 1916. Fenton, generally acknowledged as a pioneer of war photography, was interested in its relationship to art and was the first secretary of the Royal Photographic Society. At the invitation of the War Office and with the backing of the publishing firm of Agnews he went as a civilian to the Crimea in 1855 in the expectation of producing material to counter William Howard Russell's reports to *The Times* of the appalling conditions during the winter of 1854–5 after the British defeats in the battles of Balaclava, Alma, and Inkermann. Ernest Brooks was an ex-*Daily Mirror* professional who was given military rank as an honorary Second Lieutenant and officially commissioned as a photographer as the War Office reluctantly conceded to the demands of the press and propaganda organizations for more information from the front. Fenton's cameras were cumbersome, tripod-mounted affairs taking glass negatives which had to be coated with the appropriate chemicals on the spot and developed in a mobile darkroom immediately after exposure. In contrast Brooks, with his hand-held equipment and pre-prepared glass negatives, could wander all day at will, limited only by the number of glass plates he could carry. Fenton's slow wet-plate technique meant that his photographs needed carefully arranged subjects with adequate time and light for the long exposure at a site convenient for his van. Brooks, although his negative emulsion was slow by today's standards, could take advantage of far more opportunities and, with a choice of shutter speeds, could record them. In Fenton's work his subjects were always very conscious of the camera (*plate b*); in Brooks' they might be unaware that they had been photographed (*plate c*). The photographer in the Crimea expected to market his work only after his return to Britain either by reproduction through the engraving process in the press, or in exhibitions and sets of prints for sale, but the man on the Western Front was disappointed if his work did not appear within days in the illustrated press. Fenton worked on his own covering an army of fewer than 100,000 men engaged in a conflict remote from Britain. Brooks was one of several, although never very many, official photographers attempting to cover the greatest concentration of British forces ever assembled in a struggle so close that the noise of the guns on the Western Front could be heard across the Channel. But despite the apparent differences the problems for both men remained the perennials of professional war photography; access to the battlefield, mobility on it, and the reproduction of the work accomplished. The intervening years had achieved great technical advances but they could not solve the basic problems. During the First World War a new one was added; the increasing apparatus, both military and civilian, for the control of information from the front.

During the First World War it was for the first time possible for people to see and read about a major conflict more or less as it happened. The spread of literacy and the development of communications during the nineteenth century meant that news reached a much greater proportion of the population than ever before and the newspapers were the most important media of the day. Previously reported wars had been exciting diversions in national life and despite the occasional blunder the skirmishes of Empire had, for the most part, been seen as tales of adventure and heroism. Serious consideration of

(*a*) The Crimean War photographer Roger Fenton and his travelling photographic darkroom 1855. Science Museum.

(*b*) A carefully posed group of officers in the Crimea 1855. Roger Fenton, Q 71114.

the relationship between the leadership and a population compelled to alter profoundly its mode of life and to offer a continuous sacrifice over a prolonged period had entered neither military nor political thinking. In any case the science of analysing and understanding the influence and motivation of mass human behaviour simply did not exist. The First World War saw an enormous extension of the role of the state in the life of the individual and a definitive shift away from old liberal values of *laissez-faire*. To begin with, deliberate organization of the war effort went against the grain of the traditions of government but as the demands of the struggle multiplied the politicians found themselves assuming increasingly powerful direction on many counts of which control of the press and the management of official propaganda were but two.

Although written and visual information from the battlefronts became more controlled than ever before, in many ways this was not a planned or directed growth but a response to circumstance and the result of manoeuvring by different factions within the military, the government, and the press. The photograph as a news item was a relatively recent development in journalism and the profession of specialist press photographer a new phenomenon. Recent wars had been fought either in far-away countries or without British involvement which meant that there were no precedents for professional photography of a struggle close at hand of overwhelming importance to the nation. By 1914 technical developments in printing and photography meant that the potential existed for a greater supply of photographs than ever before.

It had become possible to earn a living as a press photographer because of the coincidence of a revolution in newspaper printing and a dramatic improvement in photographic emulsions which began in the 1880s. Previously, photographs could only be reproduced by being redrawn and printed using engraving techniques. The results were more akin to a line drawing and could show only extremes of black and white. What was needed was a process which could show the different shadings or 'half-tones'. In the 1880s it was discovered that this could be done by projecting photographs through a screen which broke up their solid blocks of colour into tiny dots. Because of the eye's limited resolving power, the dots, which were grouped according to the original densities of black and white, created the necessary illusion of shades of grey. Transferred by mechanical means to the printing block the process allowed the apparent reproduction of a full range of tones through a medium which used only black ink and white paper. The result was both cheaper in labour and closer to the original than previous methods.

But the press was a conservative industry and although photographic illustrations became prominent in the many new titles launched around the turn of the century, photography in newspapers was usually identified with the cheap end of the market. The *Daily Mirror* founded by Lord Northcliffe in 1903 was the first and most popular of the illustrated dailies. In contrast the weekly magazines such as *The Illustrated London News* and *The Sphere* with greater leisure for preparation prided themselves on their quality of reproduction and appealed to a better-off audience. During the war new serial publications, of which *The War Illustrated* was the most popular, were launched and aimed to present a pictorial narrative of the struggle. The war greatly enhanced the importance of photographs as news material and the press responded, although it was slow to give up its literary traditions.

The same period had also seen crucial technical developments in photography. In the 1880s the introduction of pre-prepared or dry-plate negatives freed the photographer from his travelling darkroom. Instead of having to cope with wet and volatile chemicals on site the new dry plates held the photographic emulsion in stable suspension ready for use, after which they could be developed at leisure. With faster shutters, improved exposure times, and better lenses they meant that the photographer could jettison his tripod and, using a hand-held camera, enjoy a new-found mobility. By 1914 the equipment of a professional photographer enabled him to concentrate on taking his

(*c*) British troops, unaware of the camera, receiving dinner rations from field kitchens in the Ancre area during the battle of the Somme, October 1916. British official, Ernest Brooks, Q 1582.

(*d*) Ernest Brooks, first and longest serving of the First World War official photographers, with his Goerz Anschutz camera on the Western Front *c.* 1917. British official, Ernest Brooks collection, Q 24087.

pictures rather than on the technical complexities of the process. It became practical for him to go in search of events and to take a range of photographs which could show the spontaneous and unexpected. His work had a realism which the most careful drawing lacked and when reproduced by the half-tone process carried especial status as direct 'evidence'. The specialist, the professional press photographer, emerged and by the outbreak of war was recognized as a craftsman in his own right.

The cameras used by the official photographers during the First World War were typical of the types favoured by professionals and gave them considerable freedom of movement and excellent technical quality. They divided into four main categories; hand-held folding plate, single lens reflex, panoramic, and field cameras. One of the standard press cameras of the day, the hand-held folding plate Goerz Anschutz, was particularly suited to war photography because of its robust, compact construction. It had a simple viewfinder on top of the body which meant that the photographer sighted at eye level, a

(*e*) The Goerz Anschutz folding plate camera with two holders (known as double dark slides) for its 5 × 4 inch negatives and its carrying case. MH 29865.

(*f*) An official photographer working for the Australian Imperial Force, Herbert Baldwin, looking down at the viewing screen of a single lens reflex camera fitted with an extra long lens on the Western Front, December 1916. Australian official, E(AUS) 222.

definite advantage in warfare where personal safety might depend on remaining inconspicuous, and its slim shape when its lens was folded was easy to carry. It was available in various formats but the war photographers normally used the five by four inch negatives which were not too cumbersome but gave a good size of image for reproduction. The glass negative plates were quite heavy but it was considered perfectly possible to carry at least a couple of dozen for a day's work. This was made easier if the individual plate holders were replaced with paper envelopes such as the popular Mackenzie Wishart type.

An alternative choice was a single lens reflex camera such as the American manufactured Auto Graflex, which had been developed commercially just after the turn of the century. This had the advantage of a more sophisticated focusing device using a glass screen on top of the camera body on to which the image was projected using the mirror of the reflex system. However, it was bulkier than the folding plate type and usually had to be used at waist level in order to look down at the focusing screen, an inconvenient combination for front-line photography. The popular Auto Graflex had the advantage of a second mirror in the focusing screen which could be locked in position allowing the camera to be used at eye level and the reflex system meant that the photographer saw exactly what his plate negative would record. Most professionals liked to work at a wide aperture close to their subjects in a good light in order to bring their foreground into strongly contrasted relief which made for good reproduction and this influenced their photography in the battlefield.

A recurring problem in war photography was to convey the scale of events and two very different methods were occasionally tried as alternatives to the standard press cameras; either small panoramic or very large field cameras. The former had lenses which pivoted through a wide angle and caught the image on narrow rectangular negatives. Ernest Brooks and the Canadian official photographer, William Rider-Rider, both used a Kodak Panoram No 4 which recorded an arc of 142 degrees on $3\frac{1}{2} \times 12$ inch roll-film. Panoramic cameras were not very expensive and as much for the amateur market as the professional. For large static shots a 'field' or 'view' camera such as the Houghton Sanderson could be used. This had the oldest viewing system of all; the user looked at a screen directly in line with the lens and saw the entire field of vision, hence the name for the type. The Sanderson had, by putting its lens panel on four supporting arms which pivoted on an extending panel in the base, been given the full range of rise and fall, swing and tilt movement necessary to correct aberrations of the lens. It was one of the most versatile cameras of the day and available in a wide range of medium to large negative sizes. These four were only the main types of cameras used. A wide choice existed within each category and, in addition, photography had been so extended that it was possible to take pictures in a stereo format using cameras with twin lenses, in interiors using primitive magnesium flash powder for illumination (*plate h*), and even in colour through the autochrome

process which used dyed grains of starch to give a genuine if rather gently coloured result.

But since the 1890s photography had been not only the province of the professional or the scientifically minded amateur, it had become available on a mass basis in a cheap and reliable form. The American George Eastman invented the first small Kodak camera taking roll-film in 1888 and refined and improved it to set the standard for the amateur market. The introduction of roll-film with its multiple exposures and light weight was a boon to the user, giving him greater capacity and freeing him from the necessity to do his own processing as Kodak offered a full range of facilities. From the 1890s onwards the range of amateur cameras, starting with the Folding Kodaks, became increasingly successful as Eastman aimed steadily towards an ever better combination of small camera and satisfactory result. Promoted with his famous slogan 'You press the button, we do the rest', the range of Folding Pocket Kodaks was introduced in 1898 and the still smaller Vest Pocket Kodaks in 1912 (*plate i*). In the former the most popular negative sizes were either quarter plate, $3\frac{1}{4} \times 4\frac{1}{4}$ inches, or postcard, $3\frac{1}{4} \times 5\frac{1}{2}$ inches, which gave a good size print without any need for enlargement, and in the latter, its tiny 127 format, either $1\frac{5}{8}$ inches square or $1\frac{5}{8}$ by $2\frac{1}{2}$ inches, made it astonishingly convenient. In some respects the amateur market was ahead of the professional, as the first

(*g*) The devastation of the battlefield of Passchendaele, taken with a panoramic camera 1917. Canadian official, William Rider-Rider, CO 2264.

camera to have a coupled rangefinder, a direct link between the lens and the viewfinder to ensure the picture was in focus, was the Kodak No 3A Autographic Special, introduced in 1916. At the outbreak of war millions of Kodak cameras and their imitations had been sold. Although the amateur generally used a smaller format than the professional, nevertheless he could sustain a perfectly reasonable technical quality.

A camera was a not uncommon part of the personal 'kit' taken to war but attitudes towards its use varied. Private cameras were equated with the keeping of diaries as being a possible security risk on active service and were therefore officially frowned on. Several attempts were made to ban them altogether but enforcement varied according to the time, place, and stance of the High Command. A camera used only for personal pleasure was less contentious than one used with a view to obtaining material for publication. For some individuals such as Mrs Elsie Knocker (later the Baroness de T'Serclaes) and Miss Mairi Chisholm who ran a first-aid post in the Belgian front line for most of the war, their possession of cameras for their own amusement was never, so far as is known, queried (*plate j*). At different times and places, private material taken by servicemen could find its way into the press, sometimes with encouragement from their superiors or at least their condonation. Amateur photography was treated as part of

(*h*) An interior probably taken using magnesium flash showing officers of the Australian 105th Howitzer battery in a dugout during the third battle of Ypres, August 1917. Australian official, E(AUS) 661.

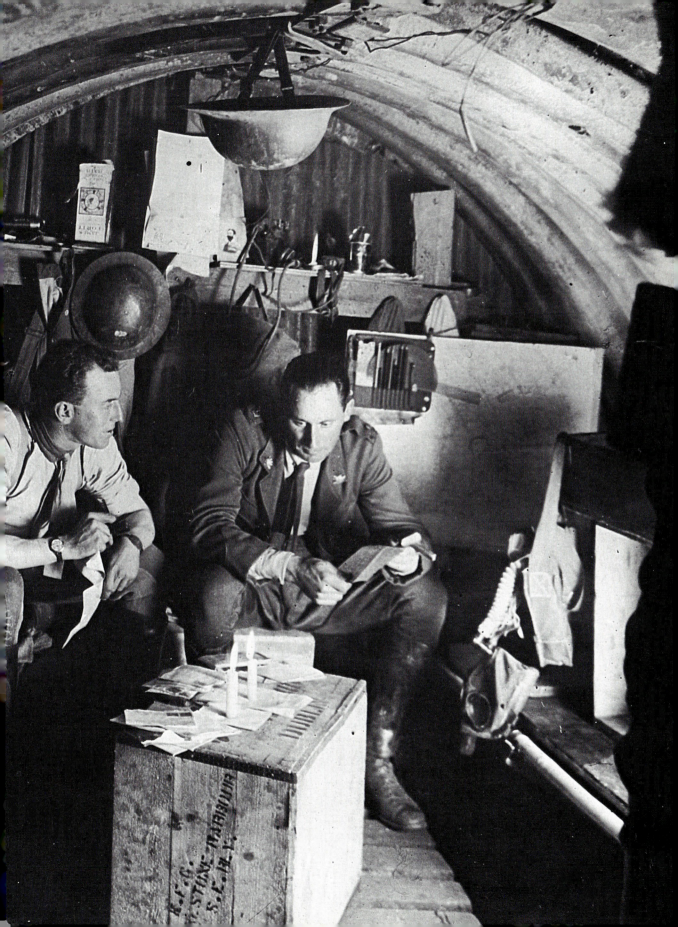

(*i*) A Vest Pocket Kodak Autographic camera of the type manufactured for the amateur market from 1915–26. MH 29843.

(*j*) An amateur photographer, Mrs Elsie Knocker (later the Baroness de T'Serclaes) holding her Vest Pocket Kodak standing with a Belgian major near the first-aid post at Pervyse, 1914. Personal photograph, Mairi Chisholm, Q 105861.

(*k*) An official home front photograph of 1918 showing a woman carter doing what had previously been regarded as a man's job. British official, Horace Nicholls, Q 31003.

the quantity of information from the battlefield for which some control seemed necessary but as with professional photography the degree applied varied considerably.

To begin with, management of 'news' was seen by political and military authorities as distinct from 'propaganda'; the need for the control of the former was deemed obvious for security, the desirability of official involvement in the untried province of the latter seemed questionable. The main civilian apparatus for censorship and dissemination of news, the Press Bureau, was set up immediately on the outbreak of war but was very much dominated by the services. In particular the Royal Navy preferred to remain as aloof as possible. The services were used to organizing their own censorship in the field but unaccustomed to meeting such a large daily demand and the first months of war were a struggle to come to terms. It was one of the dilemmas of a national war, that it was dependent on popular support which could be lost by admission of failure. The pragmatic solution found during the First World War was to invite a limited number of professionals to be part of a special elite, the official reporters, and then

to exclude all others as far as possible from the most important areas. Imposition of control was to be a matter of controlling numbers rather than content.

The Press Bureau was the obvious point for the press to bring pressure to bear when it found itself short of material and, ironically, was to play as important a part in increasing the flow of news as in its control. It admitted the need for the appointment of professional war correspondents in early 1915, applauded the greater availability of reports and photographs from the Gallipoli expedition, and in early 1916 was to be instrumental in supporting the appointment of the first official photographer to the Western Front, Ernest Brooks. Photographs were usually censored first by the military in the field and the Press Bureau remained responsible for their final censorship and distribution, but its role in the organization of their taking was assumed by the propaganda organization.

Britain, a major power secure on the world stage with the most powerful navy, the largest Empire, and one of the leading industrialized economies, had previously felt immune from criticism and above explanation of her policies to other countries. Gradually the government recognized that 'propaganda' in the sense of extensive deliberate influential activity to present and justify the country's case was concomitant with the waging of war. However, in its early stages the propaganda experiment was extremely discreet, selective, and aimed only at neutral and allied countries. The organization responsible, the War Propaganda Bureau, was set up in August 1914 and because of the secrecy surrounding it was better known by the name of its headquarters, Wellington House. It was headed by a Liberal Member of Parliament of Cabinet rank, Charles Masterman. From the first he determined to eschew sensationalism and to keep to what he called 'the propaganda of the facts'. Initially, he aimed to produce literary material for circulation to prominent people abroad in the hope of influencing bodies of opinion in Britain's favour. It was a discriminating and intellectual approach. However, at the beginning of 1916 Wellington House set up a department specifically to handle pictorial material and appointed a former journalist, Ivor Nicholson,[1] to run it. The conversion of the isolationist United States was eagerly sought by the participants in the European war and German propaganda there seemed ubiquitous and successful. It was essential that the range of the British effort should be broadened and popularized in order to contradict it, hence the move away from purely literary efforts. Supported by its parent body, the Foreign Office, Wellington House made strong representations to the War Office that the appointment of more official photographers was essential to its needs. However, its junior status *vis à vis* the established departments of state was to be a recurring problem and it made little headway. Only one more, John Warwick Brooke, was sent to the Western Front to join Ernest Brooks in 1916.

The year marked a watershed in the conduct of the war; after two and a half years victory was no nearer and the effort of sustaining the fight was becoming harder. America had still not committed herself and the home front was drained and wearied. The coalition government of the remote and apparently ineffectual H. H. Asquith was defeated and he was replaced as Prime Minister by the demagogue David Lloyd George in December 1916. More aware of public opinion at home and abroad than his predecessors, anxious to improve morale and to secure his own relations with the press, he made Wellington House into a Department of Information in February 1917. He appointed the aspiring politician and novelist, John Buchan, as Director. Later Buchan was to comment with mixed feelings on his elevation:

> I saw at close quarters the intricate mechanism which directed the War at home, one of the strangest mixtures of amateur and professional, talent and charlatanry, the patriot and the *arriviste* which history has known, with behind it the dynamic figure of the Prime Minister, generating heat and somehow turning it into power ... he was the flame at which all warmed, and many scorched, their hands.[2]

The Department did not enjoy the Prime Minister's confidence for very long. Although it established better relationships with the always wary more senior departments of state, it incurred the distrust of influential members of the press which was to lead to a further reorganization. In the meantime, Buchan, working with Masterman and the staff he had created, carried on his policy of factual propaganda. As he saw it, the stamp of 'official' was and should continue to be a guarantee of authenticity. During 1917 the scope of official photography was successfully widened to include the outer theatres of war in Egypt and Mesopotamia, the Royal Navy, and, in acknowledgement of its increasing importance, the civilian effort at home. Not all these initiatives originated from the Department, some being made in response to local circumstances in the more remote theatres, but illustrations had become an essential part of the magazines it produced for circulation abroad, and the home press was an enthusiastic customer for whatever was available. The most urgent problem remained the shortage of supply from the Western Front about which Buchan became seriously concerned.

As the dominions' contribution grew, the larger countries of the Empire sought approval for their own organizations to deal with news, propaganda material, and, by extension, photography. The first in the field, the Canadian War Records Office, was very much the brainchild of the Canadian journalist, entrepreneur, and aspirant to British inner circles of power, Max Aitken. Having sought the blessing of the Canadian Prime Minister, Sir Robert Borden, and using some of his own considerable personal funds, Aitken opened the office on 1 January 1916. As its head his declared aims were to supply publicity material and build up the written and visual record of the war for the nation. He tussled with the War Office to secure the appointment of a Canadian official photographer on the Western Front and, helped by his habit of

(*l*) Horace Nicholls, the first photographer to be officially appointed to cover the home front in 1917, has his photographic permit checked by a Sea Scout. He is equipped with a Newton and Guardia Nydia folding plate camera. British official, Horace Nicholls collection, Q 19964.

(*m*) Lord Beaverbrook at the opening of the Press Club shortly after his appointment as Minister of Information in March 1918. British official, G. P. Lewis, Q 27957.

(*n*) The Naval Censor's office at the Admiralty with the Chief Censor Admiral Sir Douglas Brownrigg seated in the centre. British official, Q 18599.

(*o*) The Ministry of Information Photographic Bureau at 12 Coventry Street taken the day before it opened to the public for the direct sale of official photographs in October 1918. British official, Horace Nicholls, Q 31117.

cultivating powerful friends, he succeeded in arranging for a man to start in April 1916 only one month after the first official British photographer. Later that year, trading on his connections and knowledge of the British press he arranged for one of the most highly reputed photographers of the *Daily Mirror* to take over. From then on Aitken played an increasingly important role not only in accumulating material for Canada but in the organization of British propaganda generally. Rewarded with a peerage for his support of Lloyd George in his bid for power at the end of 1916, Lord Beaverbrook, as he now was, had become involved with the production of official films and constantly argued for more official photographers and greater prominence for their work. His rank as head of the Canadian War Records Office enabled him to grant Canadian commissions which he used to short-circuit long-drawn-out dealings with the War Office. During 1917, as Buchan felt increasingly beleaguered and out-manoeuvred by the established offices of state at the Department of Information, Beaverbrook's influence in the organization of British propaganda grew.

The struggle to fight on during 1917 became even harder as the German submarine blockade began to take effect; the main British Army was worn down in the mud of Passchendaele on the Western Front, and the former ally, Russia, sank into revolutionary chaos. The need to rally support at all levels was urgent. Lloyd George decided to overhaul the propaganda organization once again. In February 1918 he upgraded it to a Ministry and on 4 March appointed Beaverbrook as its head with Buchan as his much-relieved subordinate. The hustle and bustle of the former's journalistic style was much resented within the new Ministry which, despite some of Beaverbrook's later claims to the contrary, provided him with an established staff and methods of work. The perennial problem of relationships with other more senior offices of state surfaced in an acute form as they regarded the parvenu Minister and Ministry with deep distrust. Beaverbrook's preferred approach of a presentation deliberately angled for maximum effect was in abrasive contrast to former ideas and many of his more ambitious plans, particularly those for the increase in the number of official photographers in the field, were only very partially realized. Frustrated and in ill-health he resigned on 21 October 1918 just before the end of the war. The Ministry did not long survive him as with the approach of peace it was seen as a potentially unseemly tool of government.

Beaverbrook's position ensured special prominence for the Canadian war effort but the other major dominion, Australia, pursued a very different line, although it also owed a great deal to a single individual. Charles Bean, a respected Australian journalist, was appointed as the official correspondent for his country to the Gallipoli expedition in 1915. Trained as a historian with an innate respect for the record in preference to the sensational, he was from the first more concerned with the long term. At Gallipoli and later on the Western Front his tall, gangling figure, apparently more suited to the study than the field, was to be seen constantly roving the battlefield seeking information. He was to be the driving force and preceptor behind the setting up of the Australian War Record Office in April 1917 and would later mastermind the painstakingly complete Australian official histories. He appreciated the importance of the visual record and not only tried to accumulate as many private photographs as possible but also argued for the appointment of an official Australian photographer on the Western Front. He succeeded in November 1916 and from then on there was at least one man attached specifically to the Australian Imperial Force.

As the war continued the idea of its permanent record gained currency. The idea of founding a National War Museum in London was first mooted in March 1917 and a Cabinet Committee formed to study the proposal. As the Empire protested at its exclusion, the title was changed to Imperial War Museum. It began active collecting of suitable artefacts and suggested that after the war the accumulations of official material including photographs should be deposited in its care. Those involved in their taking became aware of this possibility and on the home front the Museum was actively involved in their commissioning. After the Armistice as Buchan began the dismantlement of the Ministry of Information, it was agreed that the transfers should take place. On 1 January 1919 the Ministry's Photographic Bureau at 12 Coventry Street became the Museum's Department of Photographs, taking over the entire collection, the administrative staff, and some still active photographers. The material which had been sought for publicity became part of the national record.

During the war the photographers in the field were for the most part remote from the arguments and acrimony between politicians, civil servants, the services, and the newly established organizations concerned with the control and accumulation of information. Nevertheless these disputes had a bearing on what was possible, permissible, and publishable. The boundaries between different types of material – official, press, and private – became blurred by the practical difficulties of photography itself and in the end all were used as a contribution to the contemporary and long-term account of the war.

(*p*) The Australian official correspondent and historian, Captain Charles Bean, affectionately dubbed 'Anzac Charley' on the Western Front in 1917. Australian official, E(AUS) 246.

2

UNCERTAIN BEGINNINGS:
The Western Front and Gallipoli 1914–15

The Western Front

It had been assumed for past decades that the main role of the small professional British army was to defend the outposts of Empire rather than engage in a continental war against huge conscript armies. Nevertheless on 4 August 1914 Britain committed herself to war in Europe and the first units of her small Expeditionary Force landed in France three days later. Its role was to support French and Belgian efforts to halt the cracking pace of the German advance. Its first four divisions took up position at Mons in Belgium and found themselves facing the whole weight of the German First Army on 23 August. The enemy attacks petered out against the extraordinary co-ordination of British rifle fire but as the line of the Allied armies wavered the position became untenable. In a series of running battles that autumn the main thrust of the German attack across northern Europe towards Paris was deflected as the opposing armies tried frantically to outflank each other and edged closer and closer to the Belgian coast. The war of movement ended as they ran out of space. The lines of opposing forces now stretched from the English Channel to the Swiss border. They consolidated their positions and began to dig the trench systems which became characteristic of the Western Front. The conundrum of this type of warfare was soon amply demonstrated; in a well-protected position the advantage lay always with the defenders. The attackers, advancing exposed across no-man's-land, had no adequate protection against the fusillades of shells and bullets and colossal bloodshed was inevitable. By the end of 1915 Britain had suffered over 490,000 casualties of whom about 185,000 were reported as dead or missing. The much larger French army had lost nearly two million men. Although much of the detail of war was seen in the photographs taken and published at the time, there was little indication of its cost. The sheer lack of professional photographers, the adherence of those who gained access to contemporary publishing standards, and considerations of military security combined with natural reticence in both amateur and professional in dealing with the horrific.

In the initial flurry any official organization of a system of reporting broke down in the face of the ban imposed on 11 August at the personal wish of the Secretary of State for War, Field Marshal Lord

(a) The Scots Guards marching out of their depot at the Tower of London, August 1914. Professional photograph, Christopher Pilkington, Q 57104.

Kitchener. His view naturally prevailed, although there were members of the military hierarchy who shared neither his obsessive concern for secrecy nor his conviction that his own authority was always paramount. In spite of him there remained a certain amount of scope on the Western Front for photography and its publication by both professionals and amateurs.

Through the personal initiative of one of its officers,[1] a professional photographer, Sergeant Christopher Pilkington of the Artists' Rifles, was attached to the 2nd Battalion of the Scots Guards from September 1914 until January 1915. The appointment seems to have been a purely private arrangement made by the battalion with a view to securing its own visual account and was accepted by the military

(b) Civilians on the ramparts of Ypres watch the bombardment of the city in October 1914. Professional photograph, Christopher Pilkington, Q 57319.

hierarchy as such. Pilkington recorded assiduously their preparations for war, their cheerful departure from the base at the Tower of London, their hasty preliminary training exercises at Lyndhurst in Hampshire, their embarkation for Zeebrugge on 6 October, and their involvement in the first battle of Ypres in October and November. He noted in his diary[2] that his large and small format cameras helped him to make the most of opportunities. Based in Ypres he took many photographs of the town including the Cathedral, which was then just beginning to show the effects of bombardment. He saw civilians observing the fighting as they might have done in earlier wars from the town ramparts, unaware that in this kind of struggle there would soon be no room for spectators. Further up the line he found men in improvised shelters and hastily dug trenches sheltering from the modern weapons of shell fire and machine gun.

But although Pilkington had remarkable free range, one of the fundamentals of photography in the First World War was apparent; to take pictures which showed fighting in the sense of actual encounters with the enemy was very nearly impossible. At the moment of

THE SPHERE

AN ILLUSTRATED NEWSPAPER FOR THE HOME   With which is incorporated "BLACK & WHITE"

Volume LXI. No. 801 {REGISTERED AT THE GENERAL POST OFFICE AS A NEWSPAPER} London, May 29, 1915.   Price Sixpence.

Copyrighted in the U.S.A.   DRAWN BY F. MATANIA, SPECIAL ARTIST OF "THE SPHERE" IN FRANCE, 1915

HOW THE GAS DEVIL COMES—"THE THICK GREEN MIST CAME ROLLING TOWARDS THE PARAPET"

(c) A typical artistic representation of the front line: the effect of one of the first gas attacks at Ypres drawn by F. Matania and published on the cover of *The Sphere*, 29 May 1915.

How Tommy Atkins Finds his Way in France : *A Direct Camera Picture. November,* 1914.

"À GAUCHE, MONSIEUR, PRÈS DU MOULIN"—A FRENCH PEASANT ASSISTS THE BRITISH SOLDIER

(*d*) 'How Tommy Atkins finds his way in France': a characteristic presentation in style and subject of what professional photographers could take on the Western Front in 1914–15. *The Sphere*, 5 December 1914.

attack there was no room for supernumeraries, the enemy was rarely actually seen and certainly not close enough to photograph. Pilkington took some varied scenes during the first battle of Ypres showing the Scots Guards' transport, roll-calls, and ration issues but he could only hope to be on the periphery of the fighting. In any case his instructions seem to have been that he should be more concerned with recording the roll of honour of the regiment than its battles. He went to some trouble to photograph as many of its graves as possible but the results were some of the least interesting of his work, the strength of which lay in its comprehensive account of a battalion's experiences in the early days of the war and the manner in which it evoked the continued existence of old attitudes alongside new methods. It is not clear exactly why his appointment ended in January 1915 but there are hints in his diary that stricter enforcement of the regulations about photography in the battle area meant he had to return home.

Initially the outbreak of war was seen as providing exciting opportunities for the press but once banned from the Western Front there was little it could do except rely on the brief official communiqués and occasional fuller accounts issued by General Headquarters. Some reporters and photographers attempted to hang around the fringes of the battle area but found that without military co-operation it availed them little. Such photographs as were taken tended to be innocuous views of the ordinary British infantryman, 'Tommy Atkins' (*plate d*), and when published were accompanied by descriptions of his general resourcefulness and fitness, which combined with his cheerful patriotism to give a thoroughly optimistic glow. In spite of the lack of supplies several new photographic serials started including *The Illustrated War News* and *The War Illustrated*.

Faced with a serious shortage of material from its own forces the illustrated press sought alternatives from foreign agencies, improvised with old stock, used the drawings of artists whose imagination could take them right into the front line, and, eventually with some success, sought photographs from the soldiers themselves. While personal photography was not encouraged, much depended on the attitude of those in command of individual units. In the continued absence of professional opportunity, the press even mounted competitions to attract submissions from men serving on the Western Front. As a matter of course material could not be published without the approval of the censor but apart from the obvious caution of naming neither units nor exact locations there seems to have been no great difficulty in clearing such photographs. For example, the Christmas truce of December 1914 was a remarkable occasion which those involved naturally tried to record if they could. On 25 December along the length of the line on the Western Front soldiers left their trenches and fraternized in no-man's-land. A private in the London Rifle Brigade stationed near Armentières, J. Selby Grigg, described the extraordinary events in a letter home:

when Turner and I and some of our pals strolled up from the reserve trenches after dinner, we found a crowd of some 100 tommies of each nationality holding a regular mothers' meeting between the trenches. We found our enemies to be Saxons. ... I raked up some of my rusty German and chatted with some of them. None of them seemed to have any personal animosity against England and all said they would be jolly glad when the war was over. Turner took some snaps with his pocket camera.[3] (*plate e*)

Quite a number of the private photographs taken were passed to the press for publication and the event was regarded as being in the chivalrous tradition of war.

Lieutenant R. C. Money of the 1st Battalion Cameronians (Scottish Rifles) was typical of those who took general photographs of their units for their personal satisfaction and with their superiors' approval sent selections for publication. The Cameronians were one of the very early units to arrive in France, having left Glasgow on 8 August and arrived at Le Havre on the 16th. Money's photographs follow the stages of their departure, their advance across France often along pleasantly wooded lanes in the sunshine of late summer and their involvement in the mobile fighting and the stabilization of the line in Flanders. His was very much an insider's view as he snapped his friends eating outside their dugout, busy digging the increasingly complex trench systems, and being instructed in and using the new equipment of war such as the machine gun and gas mask. *The Sphere* used several of his pictures to stress the themes of security, comfort, and safety at the front; for instance his picture of an 18-pound field gun in a concealed shelter in the Armentières sector was published on 16 December headlined 'Protected Tommies and a Protected Gun' and captioned:

> The British soldier and the British gun are both well protected. Our soldiers at the front are now protected against the cold by sheepskin coats and our big guns are carefully protected by cleverly designed concealments from the enemy's observation. The picture shows a group of field artillery officers round a big gun in France. They all look quite snug. (*plate h*)

Serving soldiers could always document their own version of war but occasionally personal collections provided visual evidence of a unique type of experience. From November 1914 until spring 1918 two British women, Mrs Elsie Knocker and Miss Mairi Chisholm, ran a first-aid post in the Belgian front line. Both very young, but with driving and nursing experience, they came as part of a volunteer flying ambulance corps to help the beleaguered Belgian army. Deciding that what was most needed was swift initial treatment of casualties, they chose a site for their first-aid post as close to the front line as possible. The cellar of a damaged house in Pervyse offered rudimentary security and here Mrs Knocker took charge of the nursing while Mairi Chisholm

(*e*) The Christmas Truce 1914: German soldiers of a Saxon Regiment fraternizing with a member of the London Rifle Brigade (left in greatcoat) near Armentières. Personal photograph, R. Turner, Q 11718.

(*f*) Mairi Chisholm having fun with soldiers on a see-saw near the first-aid post of Pervyse 1915. Personal photograph, Baroness de T'Serclaes, Q 105968.

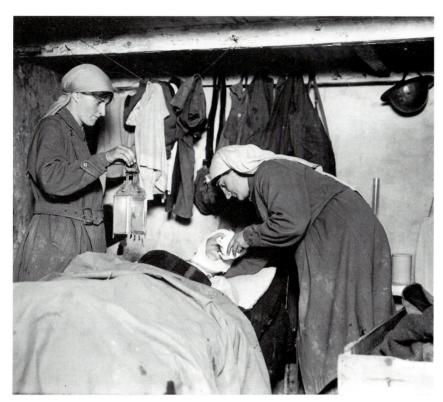

(*g*) Mairi Chisholm (holding light) and the Baroness de T'Serclaes attending to a wounded Belgian soldier in their third advanced first-aid post at Pervyse 1917. British official, Ernest Brooks, Q 2676.

(*h*) An 18-pounder field gun manned by the Scottish Rifles in a concealed shelter in the Armentières sector, published in *The Sphere* 16 December 1914. Personal photograph, R. C. Money, Q 51542.

drove their ambulance to collect the wounded. She described these journeys:

> Taking wounded to hospital fifteen miles back at night was a very real strain – no lights, shell-pocked pavie roads, mud-covered, often under fire, men and guns coming up to relieve the trenches, total darkness, yells to mind one's self and get out of the way, meaning a sickening slide off the pavie into deep mud – screams from the stretchers behind one and thumps in the back through the canvas [of the ambulance] – then an appeal to passing soldiers to shoulder the ambulance back on to the pavie. . . .[4]

Forced to move twice by bombardment, they worked on undaunted and became national heroines, 'the Women of Pervyse'.

Both had cameras and kept diaries; but although the latter have such vivid descriptions of terror, their pictures, taken when they could relax, tend to show a much lighter atmosphere; each other framed by the peculiar geometry of the ruins, with the various pets they adopted, Elsie Knocker's wedding day when she married a Belgian pilot and became the Baroness de T'Serclaes, visitors, increasingly distinguished as their fame grew, who came for tea, or high jinks on an improvised see-saw with Belgian soldiers (*plate f*). They were too busy to photograph the main purpose of their daily round, and in this sense their own visual record is incomplete. Nevertheless it adds considerably to the understanding of these two remarkable women. They were visited by Ernest Brooks in 1917 who with professional skill composed official photographs incorporating all the elements of their daily life; the patients, the bare interior of their post, and their ambulance (*plate g*). His work provided a comprehensive view in a form suitable for publication. It also highlighted the difference between the private and the professional photographer; the former rarely had leisure in the heat of war to photograph what he or she was most concerned with, while the latter used his training to compose a photograph from which information about people and their circumstances could be absorbed.

For the first twenty months on the Western Front, photography of the main British war effort was haphazard, done either by amateurs or professionals such as Christopher Pilkington appointed through a personal initiative without publication in view. Professional photographers were excluded from the prime area of interest. For the British press this meant making do with far more meagre material than it had hoped for, but did not deter it from a consistent theme of aggressive confidence in the spirit of the British army against an inferior. Although publications such as the *Daily Mirror*, *The Sphere*, and *The War Illustrated* all made much of the camera's ability to 'witness' war and stressed the publication of 'direct camera pictures', on occasion they felt the need to explain their difficulties; an issue of *The War Illustrated* on 14 November 1914 declared:

> From the pictorial point of view modern warfare lacks much which the battlefields of the past provided. Soldiers today are fighting

enemies on the continent whom they never see. . . . For this reason the great mass of photographs which reach us do not show actual hostilities in progress.

The amateur was bound by his circumstances to produce a compilation on a small scale, and although that might include the exceptional historic moment such as the Christmas truce, he could not attempt the comprehensive. Personal photographs such as those taken by Lieutenant Money and the women of Pervyse were expressive of their takers' personalities as well as of their environment and, like many such, emphasized courage and gaiety rather than the price in terms of strain and loss. The visual record of the early part of the war was constrained by the military refusal to admit publicity as a consideration in waging it and by the limitations of individual experience. Yet the implicit assumptions of patriotism and bravery revealed in so many personal photographs was in itself indicative of the mood of the period and, in the absence of any alternative, made them suitable publicity material.

Gallipoli

At the beginning of 1915 attention was temporarily distracted from the Western Front by the attempt to open another theatre of operations in the eastern Mediterranean. At the outbreak of war it had been assumed that the crucial role in any struggle would be played by the most powerful navy in the world, the Royal Navy. The First Lord of the Admiralty, Winston Churchill, believed that the entry of the Ottoman Empire as Germany's ally provided the yearned-for opportunity. Since the Turkish declaration of war on 1 November 1914, the Dardanelles Straits, the narrow waterway linking the eastern Mediterranean with the Black Sea, had been closed to Allied shipping. An alluring prospect beckoned; if the Royal Navy could force a passage the way would be clear to Constantinople, Russia would be able to use her warm-water ports in the Black Sea, some of the wavering allegiances of the various nationalities in the Balkans might be secured, and Turkey might be forced out of the war altogether. It was an audacious gamble played without adequate preparation or support. In February and March 1915, ships of the British and French navies tried and failed to bombard their way through the Straits. An army, the Mediterranean Expeditionary Force, commanded by General Sir Ian Hamilton and which included British and French units and the newly formed Anzac Corps (Australian and New Zealand Army Corps) was dispatched hurriedly to help. It mustered in Egypt with its headquarters in Cairo and then sailed from Alexandria with the intention of using the islands, Lemnos and Imbros, off the Turkish coast, as its forward bases for a landing on the Gallipoli peninsula on the northern shores of the Straits. The attempt was made on 25 April and a small beach-head secured at great cost with considerable muddle on both sides. The Turks repelled all efforts to increase its area. A major new initiative was mounted in August with increased forces but incompetent overall co-ordination meant that despite some heroic fighting the Expeditionary Force was unable to break through. In the hot Mediterranean summer, sickness as well as battle casualties seriously depleted the fighting strength. By autumn the only sensible course seemed to be evacuation and eventually the order was given for withdrawal. On 8 January 1916 the last units left.

Photography at Gallipoli was much more profuse than on the Western Front; an experiment was made with official photography, professionals, or at least war correspondents with cameras, were admitted, and a very relaxed attitude prevailed towards the use of private equipment. A former war correspondent himself, Churchill was naturally more sympathetic to requests for reportage and, supported by General Hamilton, used his considerable powers to persuade Kitchener to agree that at least some representatives of the press should accompany the force.

As the planned expedition was predominantly naval, its official photographer was appointed more or less through the personal initiative of the Chief Naval Censor, Admiral Sir Douglas Brownrigg, who grew impatient with the protracted discussion. Ernest Brooks, a former *Daily Mirror* photographer, was already in the Navy as a member of the Royal Naval Volunteer Reserve Anti-Aircraft Corps and willing to offer his professional skill. As an official photographer he was assured of co-operation from the authorities but on transfer he had no actual rank. His official photographs were guaranteed a wide circulation rather than being the property of only one newspaper or agency. The formalities were completed on 13 April and two days later Brooks left London for Gallipoli.

As a professional Brooks understood exactly how to compose appealing publishable photographs; his shot of three absurdly young midshipmen, two of whom had won the Victoria Cross for gallantry during the landings, was published in the *Tatler* on 25 August with a laudatory description. Headlined 'A Very Great Adventure' it went on:

> Three cheerful middies off for a beano. Comparisons are always odious, but perhaps we may be allowed to remark that perhaps of all her gallant sons, Jack Tar has the warmest corner in the heart of the British public; and, further, without any consideration, we believe the 'middy' is the most popular unit of that most popular service. Affectionately referred to by his superiors as a 'wart' he has appropriately helped to save the face of the service by his gallantry in the terrible landing on the peninsula. . . .

Brooks' photographs showed the dramatically large weapons of war, satisfactory 'bags' of prisoners, and deferential portraits of socially notable officers and the High Command. The fierceness of winter caught the depressed force by surprise and Brooks took some telling pictures of the ill-equipped and frost-bitten soldiers making do in

improvised shelters (*plate k*). However press coverage of the final months and the evacuation tended to try to salvage victory from defeat; some of Brooks' panoramic photographs of the camps taken in the relatively calm conditions of months before were used to imply the orderliness of the retreat (*plate l*). The content of Brooks' photographs paralleled exactly that of other professional photographers at Gallipoli and there was no attempt to establish an official point of view but only to increase the supply to the press. Although his work seemed to be generally approved, Rear-Admiral Sir Douglas Brownrigg failed to convince the Admiralty that the experiment was worthwhile and might be continued.

For the record Brooks' official photographs were complemented by a considerable quality of amateur work, in particular that done by Australians and New Zealanders with the Anzac Corps. The corps had its own correspondents but no official photographers, and the historical record benefited considerably from the relaxation of regulations about private photography. The first official Australian correspondent, Captain Charles Bean, had from the beginning been conscious of the

(*i*) Three midshipmen on shore leave on the island of Imbros, the forward base for Gallipoli: George Drewry VC, Wilfred Malleson VC, and Greg Russell. Their Victoria Crosses were awarded for bravery during the landings; the picture was published with a fulsome tribute in the *Tatler*, 25 August 1915. British official, Ernest Brooks, Q 13406.

(j) A 60 lb battery in action at Gallipoli, published by the *Daily Mirror*, 17 July 1915. British official, Ernest Brooks, Q 13340.

importance of securing as comprehensive an account as possible. Virtually single-handed he set out to obtain the necessary materials. He made a point of always following the actions as closely as possible and questioning many of the participants. He regarded his personal camera as an important adjunct to his activities, using it to show trench positions, the daily chore of organizing supplies on the almost waterless peninsula, and with a patriot's and scholar's delight in the unquenched spirit and absurdities of war, anomalies such as a game of cricket being played on a beach barely out of range of shell fire (*plate o*). Bean's written reports were highly regarded but his photographic activities were very much his own affair. It was at Gallipoli that he began the collection of personal photographs which was to be the foundation of the Australian War Memorial collection. With their careful descriptions these documented important events such as the landings of 25 April, the aftermath of bloody encounters such as Lone Pine on 8 August (*plate n*), and showed the living conditions of the soldiers, with their dugouts perched precariously on the hillside and

all the difficulties of transport and supplies. In some of them the sense of commitment and common pride was striking. Taken without the conscious seeking after a publishable photograph which characterized Brooks' work and lacking his technical consistency, they were nevertheless important historical records and sometimes powerful images as well. A considerable number of professional photographs showing the Anzacs were published in the British press and together with the correspondents' reports began to suggest an altered relationship between the mother country and her colony. At the beginning the War Office had supposed that there would be little difference between the 'colonial' and 'native' troops supplied by the Empire; both would require to be officered by the British and integrated with the British forces. No allowance had been made for an assertion of national identity and independence. At Gallipoli the Anzacs had proved to have ample measure of both plus outstanding fighting spirit. The published photographs reflected the changed perception; at the end of April a caption in *The Illustrated London News* described the landings: 'raw

(k) Frost-bitten soldiers lying on straw in shelters constructed of biscuit boxes at a store dump at Suvla, Gallipoli, November 1915. British official, Ernest Brooks, Q 13644.

(*l*) A panoramic photograph of Gully Ravine, Gallipoli, taken in the relatively peaceful days of September 1915 and published in the *Daily Mirror* on 13 January as part of its coverage of the evacuation. British official, Ernest Brooks, Q 13400A.

SUVLA BAY : Close Quarters on the Sea's Edge.

LANDING CONDITIONS ON THE GALLIPOLI PENINSULA—A SCENE BY THE WATER'S EDGE AT SUVLA BAY

(*n*) Australian dead on the parapet of Lone Pine trench system after the fighting at Gallipoli on 8 August 1915. Personal photograph, H. Jacobs, HU 53359.

(*o*) The only game of cricket ever played on the Gallipoli peninsula at the aptly named Shell Green, 7 December 1915. Personal photograph, Charles Bean, HU 53370.

(*m*) A typical scene on the narrow beaches of the Gallipoli peninsula: troops waiting to advance from Suvla Bay, probably *c.* September 1915. Professional photograph, *The Sphere*, 11 December 1915.

Colonial troops in those desperate hours proved themselves worthy to fight side by side with the heroes of Mons and the Aisne, Ypres and Neuve Chapelle.'

The first year and a half of the war on the Western Front and at Gallipoli was recorded chiefly by amateur photographers. Their collections offered a valuable but inevitably personal view of war and they sometimes recorded subjects, such as corpses, deemed unfit for publication. But unless assembled in fairly large quantities, their photographs could not be comprehensive. However, in the absence of alternatives they were the chief source of supply to the press from the Western Front. Struggling for quantity in its coverage of Flanders and Gallipoli, the illustrated press frequently found that the only available resources were foreign photographs, old material, or artistic representations of events in the front line. A disproportionate number of foreign photographs were used. None of what was published seriously disturbed the confident tone, and the success of the single official photographer at Gallipoli showed how well he melded into contemporary standards of reporting. The Australian official correspondent, Charles Bean, was virtually unique at this period in his regard for photographs as part of a comprehensive war record.

The competitions mounted by the press to attract more submissions had caused consternation at General Headquarters in France and after April 1915 only one camera per fighting unit was allowed. Few photographs survive at all of the main offensives of the rest of that year at Festubert, Aubers Ridge, and Loos, and those that do were taken, like other private photographs, on the periphery of the battlefield in moments of relaxation. They were not concerned with the horror of mounting casualties. The experiment at Gallipoli had shown that the admission of professional reporters and photographers to the battlefield was not impossible. The evacuation of all troops from the peninsula in January 1916 meant that the British effort was once again concentrated on the Western Front. Given the diminished supply of visual material, the increasing desperation of the press, and the recent successfully concluded experiment, the time was ripe for the implementation of official photography in the main theatre of war.

(*p*) Australian father (pipe smoker) and son (in front) serving together in the trenches on Walkers Ridge, Gallipoli. Personal photograph, H. V. Woods, HU 53364.

3

OFFICIAL CONTROL:
The Western Front 1916–18

The failure at Gallipoli seemed to demonstrate the futility of trying to win the war through diversionary operations and although Britain continued to devote substantial resources to operations against the Central Powers in Egypt, Mesopotamia, and other theatres, there was now little doubt that the main confrontation of forces and ultimate victory would have to be achieved on the Western Front. Straddled

across western Belgium and northern France in the area generally known as Flanders, the British army was sandwiched between the surviving remnant of the Belgian contingent in the north and the much larger French forces to the south. Its front line stretched for over eighty miles across the countryside and the total of men under arms reached well over two million. Because it lay across the obvious path to Paris it frequently bore the brunt of the fighting. The deadlock of trench warfare continued until the spring of 1918 when the Germans, greatly strengthened by the transfer of divisions from the recently closed Russian front, launched an all-out assault which came agonizingly close to inflicting defeat. It was a last attempt. Slowly the counter-attacks began and gathered momentum until by the autumn the Allies were pushing forward into new territory. An armistice was agreed and came into force on 11 November 1918.

As the most important theatre of war the Western Front saw the strictest control of information both written and visual. It was here that the greatest number of official appointments of correspondents,

(a) The first day of the Somme, 1 July 1916: a widely published photograph of an assault battalion, the Tyneside Irish, going forward at La Boisselle in the first minutes of the attack. More troops wait in the trench below the skyline. British official, Royal Engineers, Q 53.

photographers, cinematographers, and war artists was made and the ordinary press-man most rigorously excluded. Official photographers served with the British and colonial forces and although the number of men involved was small, not more than a dozen, they achieved an impressive body of work. Their successes and difficulties mirrored the progress of the war; the first were admitted to the front in the year of general optimism, 1916; they slogged on, their numbers slightly increased to cover the dominion forces, through the year of endurance, 1917; became confused and exhausted in the near defeat of early 1918, but recovered to a certain extent as victory came in sight. The problems they faced were not just those of participating in the military effort but were compounded by the shifting network of relationships behind them, between the military administrator and soldier, the censor, the propagandist, and the press, and the variously historically minded or publicity-conscious organizations involved.

1916 saw the first establishment of British and Imperial official photographers on the Western Front. The obvious choice, the only man with experience of this kind of work, Ernest Brooks, was transferred from the Admiralty to the War Office and was sent to the front as an honorary Second Lieutenant in March. He was followed by another professional press photographer, John Warwick Brooke of the Topical Press agency, in July. Warwick Brooke had been promoted from the ranks to temporary Second Lieutenant when his name was put forward by the Proprietors' Association of Press Photographic Agencies, formed to represent the interest of the trade. These appointments were achieved largely because, frustrated at its continued exclusion, the trade found support for its case within the government organization. After the disappointments and ineptitudes of the campaigns of 1915, the end of the year had seen a major reorganization of the administration of the war effort at home and in Flanders, with the appointment of Sir William Robertson as Chief of the General Staff and General Sir Douglas Haig as Commander-in-Chief of the British Expeditionary Force. One of its consequences was a much greater receptiveness to the concept of military publicity in the reorganized Intelligence section on the Western Front. The first official war correspondents had been admitted the previous year but 1916 saw great expansion, not only for the scope of their efforts but also for the admission of other categories of reporter such as photographers and cinematographers. When first the Press Bureau and then the propaganda organization at Wellington House voiced their concern that visual publicity for the British effort at home and abroad was being overtaken by other countries, negotiations were put in hand and the appointments of the British official photographers followed. For the Canadians, Max Aitken in his capacity as head of the Canadian War Records Office, obtained permission from the War Office for a Canadian serving soldier, Harry Knobel, to act as official photographer from April 1916 onwards, and, when he fell ill in June, to replace him with the former *Daily Mirror* professional, Ivor Castle. When Charles Bean, the Australian official correspondent, arrived from Gallipoli he was disappointed to be told that if he wanted photographs he must request the services of the British. Not until the end of the year did he succeed in obtaining War Office permission for the appointment of another professional, Herbert Baldwin of the Central Press Agency, to cover Australian efforts. From late 1916 onwards another Englishman, Thomas Scales, acted as the official New Zealand photographer but concentrated very much on recreational activities. All the photographers were given commissioned status, at this stage usually in the rank of honorary or temporary second lieutenant, and their salaries paid through the government organizations concerned.

The fundamental change in attitude was demonstrated by the arrangements made for the coverage of the opening of the biggest offensive of 1916, the start of the battle of the Somme on 1 July. Hopes were high that with the huge numbers of volunteer recruits who had responded to the call to arms, this would be the year of 'The Big Push' and a breakthrough on the Western Front. Haig planned a massive assault preceded by an awesome weight of bombardment lasting several days. In theory the defences would be pulverized and the defenders stunned beyond hope of recovery. At 7.30 a.m. on 1 July after seven days of artillery barrage the signal to advance was finally given. Wave after wave of infantry went 'over the top' in the hot sunshine only to be beaten back by the far from prostrate Germans. Nearly 60,000 were killed, wounded, or captured on the first day alone and the advance was measured in yards rather than miles. As Ernest Brooks was the only official photographer already present, Haig's Chief of Intelligence and the officer ultimately responsible for matters relating to the press, Brigadier-General Sir John Charteris, agreed that Brooks' efforts should be supplemented by photographs taken by the branch of the army traditionally responsible for photography, the Royal Engineers, in order to produce as many as possible. They were given unheard-of facilities; on 1 July Ernest Brooks and at least three teams of Royal Engineer photographers were in the front line at Beaumont Hamel, La Boisselle, and Mametz at the moment of attack. They were able to record the final mustering of the heavily laden troops in the forward trenches, the explosion of the enormous mines just prior to the assault, and the successive waves of troops going forward.

However, the publication of these photographs reflected the expectation rather than the actuality of the battle. The extent of the disaster was only gradually realized, even by the High Command, although it was soon obvious that the much hoped-for breakthrough had not taken place. The press responded excitedly to the visual material. The bulk of coverage of 1 July reached London about a week later and was widely featured, but despite all the special arrangements, the photographs, taken without long lenses, reduced the soldiers moving forward to tiny figures in the nondescript landscape. Nevertheless, the press recognized their uniqueness and the privilege of their publication;

(b) The battle of the Somme: one of a sequence showing troops supposedly going 'over the top' taken at a training ground. The original negative shows the breech cover on the rifle of the kneeling man on the right. Canadian official, Ivor Castle, CO 874.

(c) The battle of the Somme: soldiers from Britain and the Empire leaning on a reassuringly large pile of 18-pounder shells, September 1916. Published with a suitable expression of belligerency in *The Illustrated London News* of 7 October 1916. British official, Ernest Brooks, Q 1247.

The Illustrated London News of 15 July used some taken by the Royal Engineers at La Boisselle under the heading 'The Great British Offensive' with a sub-heading 'Advancing under fire as steadily as on parade' and went on:

> The great offensive begun in the West has put to the proof the endurance and efficiency of our New Armies, and all accounts agree that they have stood the test wonderfully and fought with the utmost heroism. These remarkably interesting photographs published by official authority were taken on the field during the British advance which began on July 1....

But the facilities granted for the first day of the battle of the Somme were to prove the exception rather than the rule; nothing quite like them ever occurred again. Although the exact reasons are unclear, it was probably because the combination of optimistic expectations, the big set-piece battle, and the novelty of having war photographers available could only happen once, and afterwards the impetus behind official photography became more a matter of individual arrangements

by the photographers themselves. In any case nothing like the first day's concentration of military forces was attempted again, although when the autumn rains came, the chalky ground was churned to a sea of mud and misery by the succession of fruitless attacks which lasted until November. Each side lost in the region of 600,000 killed, wounded, or captured.

After 1 July the supply of photographs taken by the Royal Engineers gradually petered out in their concern for more military objectives. Brooks and Warwick Brooke continued the British effort and Harry Knobel, who seems not to have been granted the same special treatment on 1 July, was replaced by Ivor Castle for the Canadians. The photographers enjoyed considerable freedom of movement and judgement in deciding what to photograph. Unlike the newspaper correspondents they were not always chaperoned, but provided they obtained transport could sally forth as they wished. It was not uncommon for them to share cars with the cinematographers but there seems to have been little interchange with the war correspondents.

The photographers were fully aware of the status their work carried and that it was fundamental to official photographs that they should follow the policy of 'the propaganda of the facts' established by Charles Masterman and supported by Ivor Nicholson. With so few operators there was really no scope for any more serious direction except the regular injunctions from Wellington House for quantity and variety. The outright fake was rare but it was inevitable, given the practical difficulties of war photography and the limited number of photographs that could be taken in any one day, that a certain amount of 'scene setting' should take place. A former corporal in the 1st Lancashire Fusiliers, George Ashurst, writing in his unpublished memoirs described Ernest Brooks at work in the final week before the assault:

> It was while having a game of cards one day that we were requested
> to go out into the trench and be photographed, presumably just
> fixing bayonets ready to go over the top. It was only a few minutes
> of a job and we soon obliged, specially as the photographer ...
> promised us a tot of rum and a packet of cigarettes for our trouble.[1]

More serious was a deliberate faking of actual fighting in the front line, of which most examples could be found in the work of Ivor Castle. A sequence which purported to show troops going 'over the top' and which was widely publicized was taken in a training ground and the negatives altered to mask give-away details of the soldiers' equipment (*plate b*). Castle seems to have traded on the knowledge of Aitken's support for his role and his own reputation to achieve the sensational at the expense of the accurate and in so doing gain considerable personal publicity.

However for the most part the photographers followed a pattern which would meet accepted press requirements of providing reassurance about the success of the battle, the spirit of the troops, the supply of armaments and munitions, and the capture of prisoners.

Photographs of large groups of captives in their wire-fenced 'cages' were published as evidence of the enemy's imminent collapse if they looked depressed, or of his lack of unity if they were smiling and apparently pleased to be captured. The gentle slopes of the chalk land were blasted by the repeated bombardment and photographs, which to modern eyes evoke the devastation of war, were published as representative of proudly achieved capture. The war of attrition raised the demand for guns and shells to unprecedented levels and photographs could demonstrate apparent satisfaction with the quantity and quality supplied, although there were considerable difficulties throughout the battle on both counts. A typical case was Brooks' picture of grinning British and Empire soldiers leaning on a pile of shells which was published in *The Illustrated London News* on 7 October with the belligerent caption: 'Here we have some of our victorious gunners with a pile of shells which are to pound the German trenches level with the earth' (*plate c*). The darker side of battle, the wounded and the dead was not ignored, but photographs of the former tended to concentrate on the less badly hurt which could be published without causing grave distress, and to emphasize the physical and spiritual succour given by the medical and religious services. Photographs of the dead were taken and could be horrific, showing fly-blown and bloated corpses, but these were relatively few, as the military, the propagandists, the press, and the photographers were in tacit agreement with contemporary standards of decency that they were not fit for publication.

The photographs taken during the battle of the Somme were a landmark in the visual reporting of the Western Front. The official initiative was well established within its own limitations. Because of the scarcity of manpower and resources the photographers could not, and because of their own attitudes, which dovetailed with those of their commissioners, did not, attempt to narrate the scale of the disaster or the horrors of trench warfare; therefore in 1916 their work became part of the depiction of apparently successful endeavour.

1917 marked the emergence of the effect of the fundamental change in the basis of the war effort from volunteerism to compulsion. In 1916 the introduction of conscription and the partial nationalization of munitions manufacture began the extension of the state's remit to call on the manpower and economic resources it needed to continue the fight. A sense of determined endurance replaced the expectation of success. That year the battle on the Western Front was another epic of appalling attrition. The main offensive, the third battle of Ypres, struggled from 31 July until 10 November to advance at most five miles and secure the British army's position on the insignificant ridge which gave the battle its popular name, Passchendaele. Casualties numbered some 245,000. Five official photographers were involved and included Australian as well as Canadian appointments. The static nature of the fighting gave them opportunities for planning access to the front line. Divergences of circumstance and principle became apparent.

(*d*) The battle of Passchendaele: Rider-Rider's favourite photograph showing the 16th Canadian Machine Gun Company holding the line in November 1917. Canadian official, William Rider-Rider, CO 2246.

Ivor Castle had been recalled to London and had been replaced as Canadian official photographer by another ex-*Daily Mirror* man already serving in the British army, William Rider-Rider. He was a conscientious worker who felt strongly that his war pictures should be as authentic as possible and he described what difficulties this posed during the battle of Passchendaele:

I went up to obtain a series of pictures depicting life in the front line, accompanied by a corporal. Eventually we arrived at a post held by a dozen or so men existing in shell craters, from which they had baled the water. I took several photographs and inquired about the location of the next post. The ground was in a terrible state, all churned up. The corporal who was leading suddenly sank into the mud up to his knees. I ploughed my way to his side, and endeavoured to pull him out. It was useless. Nearby were a discarded German greatcoat, a set of equipment and two rifles, and with the help of these I finally succeeded in getting myself clear of the mud, and also my companion . . . a piece of woodwork was missing, but the camera was still in commission. We had only

gone a few yards farther when the rain came down in torrents and we returned to Ypres.[2]

His personal favourite[3] powerfully evoked the futility of Passchendaele; it showed men of the 16th Canadian Machine Gun Company holding the line in a wilderness of waterlogged shell holes in November 1917. It was published in the *Daily Mirror* with the wry comment 'A dog's life at Passchendaele ... Some [holes] are dry, but on the other hand some are not.' However, Rider-Rider found that the influence of Lord Beaverbrook meant that the emphasis was laid on getting a variety of photographs which would break the monotony of the scenes in the trenches and hence he devoted a good deal of time to such subjects as

(e) 'Très bon Canadians eh? French gleaners talking to Canadians', read the original caption of 1917. Rider-Rider posed his assistant and driver in this typical suggestion of the lighter side of war. Canadian official, William Rider-Rider, CO 1832.

fraternization with the French, concert parties, sports meetings, visits of important personages, and general ceremonial. Because of Beaverbrook's press connections Canadian material stood a better chance of being published quickly as he sidestepped as much as possible the complicated arrangements for equal distribution through the various government bodies to the photographic agencies and illustrated press. The photographs appeared rapidly and were consistently credited as showing Canadian achievement. Like many others, Rider-Rider's photographs were frequently 'interpreted' on publication to carry loaded implications. For example a photograph captioned 'A young Boche officer captured on Hill 70' was headlined 'Captured but contented' and went on: 'judging from his expression the officer in question appears more than contented with his lot and to have no regrets at leaving the struggle behind him.'

In contrast, the new entrant to the field in 1917, Australian official photography, remained chiefly concerned with the compilation of an adequate record rather than immediate publicity. Charles Bean had secured the services of Herbert Baldwin at the end of 1916 and encouraged him to produce natural and relaxed portraits of the Anzacs and all aspects of their daily round. The constitution of the Australian War Record Office in early 1917 marked the formal recognition of Bean's advocacy of a national record and gave him greater status. The limited supply of material coming from the Western Front led to the lifting of the restriction on publication of Baldwin's photographs in spring 1917, but his health broke shortly afterwards. He was replaced by two of the most interesting characters involved in official photography, Frank Hurley and George Hubert Wilkins.[4] Both Australian, they had each been involved with photography in Polar exploration, Hurley with Sir Ernest Shackleton in the Antarctic and Wilkins with Vihjalmur Stefansson in the Arctic, and had just returned to Europe. Both men were extremely tough individualists and Hurley had in addition a strong buccaneering streak. Bean had originally intended that Hurley, as the more naturally suited, would undertake publicity work and Wilkins concentrate on the historical record. In the urgency of war the distinction blurred and unfortunately the attributions to each photographer did not survive, although secondary sources indicate something of the contrast between Hurley's flamboyance and Wilkins' reticence. Bean's influence is apparent in the range of the Australian photographs which included not only the chaos and confusion of the battlefield, its death toll, and the strain on the combatants but also the more mundane details of everyday life such as health inspections, laundry work, and food preparation. There was also an unusual number of interior shots showing officers' dugouts, control posts, and medical dressing stations which indicated both men's mastery of primitive flash equipment gained on their Polar expeditions. The virtually continuous presence of Bean also ensured that the high standard of supporting documentation which he required, detailing the exact place, date, and unit shown in the photographs, was carefully

(*f*) A young German officer taken prisoner during the battle of Passchendaele described as 'Captured but contented' on the cover of *The Sphere*, 25 August 1917. Canadian official, William Rider-Rider, CO 1774.

THE SPHERE

AN ILLUSTRATED NEWSPAPER FOR THE HOME   With which is incorporated "BLACK & WHITE"

Volume LXX. No. 918.   {REGISTERED AT THE GENERAL POST OFFICE AS A NEWSPAPER}   London, August 25, 1917.   Price Sevenpence.

Canadian official picture

CAPTURED BUT CONTENTED—A GERMAN OFFICER TAKEN ON HILL 70

(*g*) Anzacs resting on the road to the trenches in December 1916: a characteristically natural photograph. Australian official, Herbert Baldwin, E(AUS) 19.

adhered to. However, Frank Hurley was aggressively determined that Australian endeavour should receive publicity comparable to the British and Canadian efforts and that he would provide the necessary material. Excited by the visual drama of war, he found it difficult to convey on film and wrote in his diary:

> Have tried and tried again to include events on a single negative but the results have been hopeless. Everything is on such a wide scale. Figures scattered, atmosphere dense with haze and smoke – shells that simply would not burst when required. All the elements of a picture were there, could they be but brought together and condensed.[5]

He tried resorting to composite photographs and combining negatives in order to convey the multiplicity of action but only succeeded in inciting the wrath of General Headquarters and Captain Bean who both felt that such tampering amounted to faking and the point of official photographs was that they should be scrupulously genuine. In the event although the composites were deemed unsuitable, other Australian photographs did appear regularly in the British press but, to Hurley's chagrin, often without specific mention of Australian achievement. However, an instance of publication of an Australian photograph showing the muddy waste of shell-cratered ground that was the ruins of the village of Passchendaele demonstrated the change in tone in war reporting from successful endeavour to persevering struggle: *The Sphere* of 24 November accompanied it with an extract from a soldier's letter:

> I cannot attempt to describe the conditions under which we are fighting. Anything that I could write about them would seem exaggerated but would in reality be miles below the truth. The whole battlefield for miles is a congested mass of sodden, rain-filled shell holes, which are being added to every moment. The mud is not so much mud as a fathomless, sticky morass.

The priorities and standards for Australian official photography on the Western Front were followed perhaps rather more readily for the rest of the war after Hurley left for Palestine at the end of 1917 and the less vehement Wilkins continued on his own.

The British official photographers faced a particularly daunting task; Brooks and Warwick Brooke continued to be the only two and they were expected to produce representative coverage of the activities of the entire British Army which now numbered over two million men, whereas the colonial photographers could concentrate on their own Corps which usually consisted of some 60,000. The military machine was becoming ever more vast and complex and, besides the battle itself, Brooks and Warwick Brooke were expected, in order to provide variety, to cover the latest peripheral activities such as the arrival of women as ancillaries, the landing of the first American contingent, the work of various exotic labour corps from the more distant parts of

(*h*) The battle of Passchendaele: an emotive interior photograph probably taken and captioned by Frank Hurley; '"How I did it." An Australian infantryman telling his comrades of an exploit is received with persiflage.' Australian official, E(AUS) 1223.

Empire, as well as the usual round of visits from royalty and other distinguished figures. Both Brooks and Warwick Brooke had been in the field almost continuously from mid-1916 and it was not surprising that they both on occasion showed signs of strain and fell back on reliable formulas.

However, it was on the second day of the third battle of Ypres, 1 August 1917, after a night of torrential rain that John Warwick Brooke took what was to become one of the most famous photographs epitomizing the nature of the conflict on the Western Front. It showed a party of stretcher bearers struggling with agonized determination to carry a wounded man through the mud and pouring rain to a casualty clearing station at Boesinghe (*plate k*). It was widely published at the time; *The Illustrated London News* of 15 September accompanied it with a quotation from a war correspondent's dispatch:

> The floating swamp is the name for a quaking morass, which gives no foothold anywhere, but heaves and oozes and bubbles in its depths as you wade through it ... those who were badly hit sank into the dreadful ooze ... the rest went on. ... Then when it was over, they turned to help their comrades who were still caught in the slime and in bodies of three or four together they pulled them out and got them safely to solid ground.

As his photograph of stretcher bearers showed, Warwick Brooke was a better candid photographer than Ernest Brooks. This was also demonstrated in their approach to the regular requirement to photograph distinguished figures; Brooks tended to conform to the accepted

practice of posed, formal shots of his subjects at their convenience as, for example, his picture of the various dignitaries, including King George V, visiting General Haig's headquarters in August 1916 (*plate m*). On the other hand, Warwick Brooke could on occasion step outside the norm to produce a revealing 'snatched' photograph such as that showing the King wearing a steel helmet and looking pensive during a visit to the front in July 1917 (*plate n*).

Brooks had a fondness for dramatic silhouettes which reproduced easily and liked taking pictures of soldiers strung out on the skyline, besides gaunt ruins of buildings or caught alone against the light. Taken as much for practical reasons as any other, they tended to be published as tributes to the anonymous heroes of the infantry. For example *The Sphere* of 20 October published two taken during one of the subsidiary battles of Passchendaele, Broodseinde, and quoted from a war correspondent's dispatch: 'I doubt if winning 1,000 yards ever called for or found finer and sterner qualities' (*plate o*).

Both men worked extremely hard to cover the range asked of them and, after the decision to found the Imperial War Museum in March

(*j*) An explicit photograph taken for the record of casualties during the last offensives; bodies of men killed near Guillemont Farm collected for burial in September 1918. Australian official, E(AUS) 4944.

(*i*) The battle of Passchendaele; a frank photograph of reaction to duty in the trenches as men of the 10th Australian Brigade sit attempting to dry themselves in front of a fire after being relieved on 14 October 1917. Australian official, E(AUS) 943.

(k) The battle of Passchendaele: stretcher bearers carrying a wounded man through the mud on the second day of the battle, 1 August 1917, one of the best known photographs of the First World War. British official, John Warwick Brooke, Q 5935.

1917, they were aware that their photographs would probably become part of the permanent record. However, although they seem to have broadened their range to include more photographs indicating the cost of war, possibly with the record in mind or in keeping with the changed tone of reporting, they simply could not produce enough to be comprehensive and satisfy demand.

In 1917 the principle of official photography became firmly established and despite the differences of outlook between the organizations which supported it, worked as well as it ever did in maintaining a supply of photographs to the press, the propaganda organization, and towards the assembly of a permanent record for Britain and her larger dominions. But in 1918 depletion of numbers caused by various reorganizations plus the sudden mobility of the war into the confusion of retreat from the German advance in the spring and then the speed of conquest in the autumn caused serious problems for the official photographers.

The dominions' efforts suffered least; for the Canadians, William Rider-Rider was able to continue very much as before, although

(*l*) A recurring image of faith and compassion: a padre gives a drink to a badly wounded soldier 1917. British official, Ernest Brooks, Q 2855.

towards the end he was constantly asked to take group pictures which were of very limited interest except to those portrayed. The indefatigable Charles Bean encouraged George Wilkins to press on but his photographs, though highly competent, lacked Frank Hurley's showmanship and sense of theatre. Each photographer now had at least some support from the ranks, usually a driver and possibly an assistant to help in the field or the darkroom, but was expected to carry out the bulk of the photography himself. The differing importance attached to photographers showed itself in their rankings; by this time the leading dominion men enjoyed captain's status while the British remained only lieutenants.

During 1917 John Buchan at the Department of Information had appealed increasingly to Beaverbrook, who was using his position as head of the Canadian War Records and as a friend of Lloyd George to become a force to be reckoned with in the propaganda effort, for help with the expansion of official photography. With his aid permission was secured for three more British official photographers; Tom Aitken and David McClellan arrived in December and Armando Consolé in

(*m*) A typical formal portrait of distinguished figures taken at Haig's headquarters during a royal visit in August 1916: the French Commander-in-Chief, General Joffre, the French President, Monsieur Poincaré, HM King George V, the Commander of the French Northern Army Group, General Foch, and the British Commander-in-Chief, General Sir Douglas Haig. British official, Ernest Brooks, Q 949.

January 1918. Unfortunately by this stage of the war any available men not already in the services were likely to be in very poor physical condition. Aitken, a professional newspaper photographer from Glasgow and Consolé, an ex-*Daily Mail* man, both suffered from bad health. The latter's appointment did not last long as he was unlucky enough to lose a leg in a shell burst in April and had to be invalided home. McClellan, who had worked for the *Daily Mirror* before the war, was transferred from the Royal Flying Corps and was rather more robust. In the event the bulk of British photography during 1918 was carried out by McClellan, Aitken, and Warwick Brooke. Ernest Brooks spent most of the final year in Italy or working on naval subjects.

Beaverbrook had infuriated the military hierarchy at General Head-quarters by using his prerogative of granting Canadian commissions to place his own man in the administration of the photographic section. However, in November 1917 it was agreed that an overall administrator was a necessity, but Beaverbrook's choice was not calculated to soothe matters. It fell on Harry Guy Bartholomew, known as 'Bart', an ardent advocate and pioneer of populist pictorial journalism, who had been appointed art director of the *Daily Mirror* in 1913 at the age of 28.[6] Impatient, energetic, and aggressive, he found the military and the ministry generally antipathetic. Although the Ministry of Information finally took formal responsibility for the photographers on the Western Front in April 1918 they remained something of a hybrid, being part of and yet not ultimately responsible to the military when on duty. Not unnaturally conflicts of priority over the availability of support services, especially transport, frequently occurred. Illness, absence, bureaucratic confusion, and practical difficulties combined to make 1918 a problematic year and arguments were swiftly overtaken by disastrous events.

The German advance launched on 21 March hurled 71 divisions against 26 of the British army which buckled and fell back towards Amiens. As successive attacks followed the situation became so grave that on 12 April Haig issued an order of the day which later became famous:

> With our backs to the wall and believing in the justice of our cause, each one of us must fight on to the end. The safety of our Homes and the Freedom of mankind alike depend upon the conduct of each one of us at this critical moment.

The Germans had achieved complete surprise and the photographers were in as much disarray as anyone. They had to do what they could to find pictures. In general the reporting of the retreat sought to emphasize the brutality of the invader and to reassure that a firm stand against him would soon be successful. The *Daily Mirror*'s use on 9 April of some of Aitken's photographs of the refugees who crowded the roads in numbers not seen since 1914 was typical; an old woman in Amiens sitting tiredly on a bench holding the leading-rein of her cow was captioned: 'This cow is all the Hun air-raiders have left the old lady' (*plate q*). Aitken seems to have had an especially sympathetic eye for the plight of the refugees and took many photographs of families with their belongings piled on carts, children forlornly seeking help, and frail old people struggling on foot along the roads.

As an antidote to the bad news there were two new themes for the photographers to add to their range. Since mid-1917 Americans had been arriving and by 1918 there were well over a million on the Western Front. Their presence was tremendously heartening to nations which had been steadily draining their resources in four years of war. Photographs emphasized their apparently universally fine physique, dash, and courage. After the alarms of the first German assault some of Aitken's photographs of American 'types' were published in *The War Illustrated* on 20 April with the obvious implication that this new blood was vital to the winning of the war. The other new phenomenon was the development of the war in the air. The Royal Flying Corps and the Royal Naval Air Service had been very much extensions of their parent services and although the duels in the air over the front had attracted much attention, the formation of

(*n*) An unusually candid portrait of King George V taken at Wytschaete Ridge during his visit to the front in early July 1917. British official, John Warwick Brooke, Q 5585.

(*o*) Two readily reproducible silhouettes taken by Ernest Brooks during the battle of Passchendaele, their drama emphasized by the accompanying text from a war correspondent's dispatch: 'I doubt if winning 1,000 yards ever called for or found finer and sterner qualities.' *The Illustrated London News*, 20 October 1917.

(*p*) A full-page feature using John Warwick Brooke's official photographs showing the novel involvement of the Women's Army Auxiliary Corps on the Western Front in 1917. *The Illustrated London News*, 18 August 1917.

THE SHARE OF THE "ARCHIES" IN THE BATTLE OF BROODSEINDE: A FINE SILHOUETTE OF A BRITISH ANTI-AIRCRAFT GUN AND ITS CREW IN ACTION NEAR FREZENBURG.

"I DOUBT IF WINNING 1000 YARDS EVER CALLED FOR OR FOUND FINER AND STERNER QUALITIES": YORKSHIRE TROOPS MOVING UP IN THE EVENING FOR THE BATTLE OF BROODSEINDE.

WOMEN IN KHAKI: THE WORK OF THE W.A.A.C. IN FRANCE.

OFFICIAL PHOTOGRAPHS.

THE WOMEN'S ARMY AUXILIARY CORPS IN FRANCE: MARCHING
IN COLUMN OF FOURS—RIGHT-WHEEL.

REPLACING MEN IN THE KITCHEN: COOKS SERVING OUT DINNERS
TO MESS ORDERLIES AT AN INFANTRY CAMP.

"WASTE NOT—": A CAMP COOK EMPTYING FAT
INTO A STOCK BARREL.

REPLACING MEN AT THE WHEEL: SOME OF THE CAR-DRIVERS OF THE W.A.A.C.
IN FRANCE.

OFF DUTY IN A FRENCH COAST TOWN: MEMBERS OF THE W.A.A.C.
COMING DOWN TO THE BEACH FOR A BATHE.

LETTERS FROM HOME: W.A.A.C. WOMEN ON THE BALCONY OF THEIR
BILLET AFTER THE ARRIVAL OF THE MAIL.

(q) The German Offensive 1918: an old woman refugee with her cow in Amiens on 28 March 1918; used in the press to show the human cost of the offensive. British official, Tom Aitken, Q 10836.

the Royal Air Force on 1 April 1918 marked its recognition as an independent force. With his former experience in the Royal Flying Corps, McClellan was an obvious choice to spend some time covering the glamorous new force.

As the tide turned towards victory McClellan was able to demonstrate his particular skill at overcoming one of the frequent criticisms of official photography, that it did not sufficiently convey the colossal scale of operations. As the British army advanced he was able by an imaginative choice of vantage points to take photographs which suggested the enormous numbers involved. After the 46th Division had on 29 September succeeded in crossing the St Quentin Canal which had formed part of the German defence system of the Hindenburg Line he photographed them massed on the bank of the canal as they waited to be addressed by their commander (*plate s*). At the clearing depot for prisoners at Abbeville he used a similar elevated view to convey the huge 'bag' of prisoners (*plate t*). However, in 1918, despite the formation of the Ministry of Information and its aspirations, British official photography remained a small operation trying to cover events on a

huge scale and further complicated by bureaucratic tangles in the background.

With the Armistice in November and the speedy dissolution of the Ministry of Information the work of the photographers ended after a brief attempt to cover the Army of Occupation in Germany. In the second half of the war, official photography was accepted as part of the apparatus of official reporting but integrated into the military hierarchy on its terms. The official photographers remained dependent on it for all their support services and information as to what was happening. Despite the shift from hostility to welcome in 1916, it remained fundamental to most military thinking that any form of reporting should be limited and occupy a lowly place in the overall scale of priorities. The result was that for all the photographers throughout the war their chief concern was to obtain sufficient quantity and variety despite their restricted numbers. There was no scope for elaborate directives but only the most basic injunction to aim for factual pictures and from 1917 onwards to consider if possible the compilation of material for the permanent record. Provided they were

(r) Officers and SE 5a Scouts of No 1 Squadron RAF at Clairmarais aerodrome, near Ypres, 3 July 1918. The group includes two Americans serving with the RAF, Lieutenants D. Knight (extreme left) and H. A. Kuhlberg (extreme right). British official, David McClellan, Q 12063.

unobtrusive the photographers enjoyed relative freedom of movement and selection. Their personal skills such as Warwick Brooke's candour and McClellan's talent for scale could emerge. With the exception of the Australians who consistently gave publication second place below the compilation of the record, choice of subject was largely determined by the publishing standards of the day. In the absence of a detailed propaganda directive, the photographers fell back on their professional training to produce the type of image they knew would be publishable. Although they had little to do with the final presentation and the emotive 'colouring' of the pictures which was done by their selection and description at the picture editor's desk, their images, with their emphasis on the mass, the variety, and the cheerfulness of the forces, could provide basic reassurance. But as the war went on and the tone of reporting changed, there was often a surprising realism in the publication and accompanying description of the photographs especially those taken during the battle of Passchendaele. However, although the cost of the fight was indicated, the basic assumption of the need to continue remained unchallenged except by very few. The photographs do not seem to have introduced any published debate on the subject although they must have helped to bridge the gap between the soldier and the civilian in the understanding of the nature of the fight.

Contradictions between the demands of publicity and record work were inherent in the development of official photography. Publicity material had to be supplied quickly and in quantity and to offer where possible attractive variety. In retrospect many such photographs have considerable historical interest but it prevented concentration on the recording and documenting of the battle, specially in the case of the British and Canadians. The photographers themselves did not believe that their role was to witness the cost of the fighting nor did they see themselves as independent observers but as patriots. The fundamental assumption of all involved that they were to report national effort and achievement held good.

(s) The final battles: the huge mass of 137 Brigade, 46 Division, on the banks of the St Quentin Canal which formed part of the German defence system, the Hindenburg Line, broken on 29 September 1918. British official, David McClellan, Q 9534.

(t) A mass of prisoners taken in the battle of St Quentin Canal assembled in a clearing depot at Abbeville on 2 October 1918. British official, David McClellan, Q 9353.

In terms of historical completeness supported by accurate documentation, the work of the official Australian photographers which owed so much to the standards set by Charles Bean formed the most careful, concentrated, and informative record of military activities. The Canadians did not have the similar advantage of being photographed mostly by their own countrymen but nevertheless, being also a single corps, were a relatively compact unit, easy to publicize and document. The British photographers were expected to cover, in all its ramifications, the biggest British army ever assembled. Most of them were older and much less fit than the front-line troops and yet they served for months at a time making regular journeys up the line. It is to their credit that they achieved as much as they did.

4

UNORTHODOX ACHIEVEMENT:
The outer theatres of war

Away from the huge static complex of the military installations on the Western Front there were far greater opportunities for all kinds of photography, but from the point of view of publishing news in the British press the distances involved created nearly insurmountable problems. Apart from the war in Flanders Britain was involved in the European campaigns in Italy and Salonika, the defence and possible acquisition of Empire in Africa and the war in the Middle East against Turkey. Fought across the Sinai desert in Egypt and Palestine and along the paths of the great rivers, the Tigris and Euphrates in Mesopotamia (approximately present-day Iraq), the war against Turkey offered scope for personal, press, and eventually most official photography. Its remoteness from the main theatre and wider range of its campaigns gave room for the unorthodox in both warfare and photography.

Egypt and Palestine

Pushed by Germany Turkey declared war on the Entente powers on 1 November 1914 and Britain's first thought was for the defence of the direct route to India via the Suez Canal. Ignoring Egypt's nominal status as a province of Turkey the Canal garrison force was hastily strengthened. But for most of 1915 Cairo was the base headquarters and Alexandria the port from which the Mediterranean Expeditionary Force launched itself to Gallipoli. There was no great difficulty about press photography of the daily round of soldiers, digging trenches in the sand, parading for review, cooking their meals in camp, and sightseeing. The material made a pleasing contrast to the Western Front and when *The War Illustrated* on 9 January published a selection showing Anzac troops it even implied a certain envy: 'To winter in Egypt as a pleasure is a rare treat, but to winter there as a duty to the Empire is something ideal.' Later, photographs of casualties from Gallipoli rather spoilt the gloss but even so these were presented as demonstrations of the effectiveness of the medical organization in a climate of immense recuperative benefit.

(*a*) A page of professional press photographs from a feature on the organization of the medical services in Egypt emphasizing the beneficial climate and good spirits of the wounded. *The Sphere*, 13 November 1915.

Private cameras abounded and although not sought for contemporary publication the photographs offer an important and often attractive documentation because of the picturesqueness of scenery and inhabitants. Many members of the British and Anzac forces

76

WITH THE WOUNDED IN EGYPT :

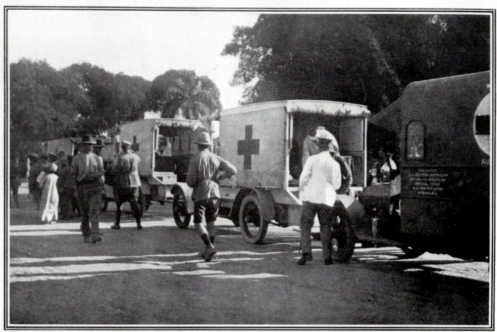

AUSTRALIAN WOUNDED IN CAIRO—Arrival of Wounded at the Australian Hospital, Cairo

"The particular motor ambulance seen on the extreme right was presented to the Western Australian section of the Imperial Force by the Hon. W. T. Loton of Perth, W.A."

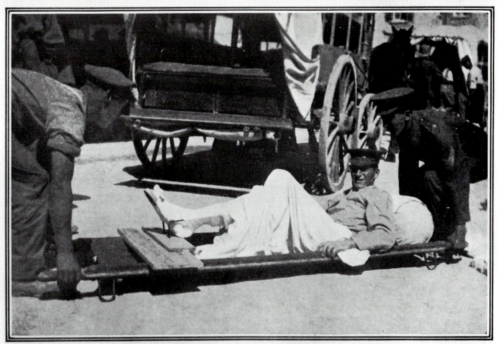

NEW ZEALAND WOUNDED IN CAIRO—Happy and Smiling, Though Wounded in the Foot

(*b*) Egypt and Palestine: the Desert Column on the march to El Arish, February 1917. Personal photograph, S. C. Byrne, Q 57770.

recorded something of the organization and transport of the Mediterranean Expeditionary Force and the routine of life in the Canal area where a great deal of time was spent digging extensive fortifications, provision against the unlikely event of a successful Turkish attack across the Sinai desert. The British withdrawal from Gallipoli in January 1916 did however pose the uncomfortable possibility of a serious Turkish threat to the Canal and the new commander, General Sir Archibald Murray, was eager to move into the desert in order to gain some room. For most of 1916 and early 1917 his troops slogged east and north, creating their lines of communications as they went. The record of that advance is mainly from officers and men with private cameras. A typical example was Colonel Stanley Byrne, commander of the 1/11 London Regiment, whose unit was attached to the newly formed Desert Column in early 1917. His photographs showed the lines of horses and camels on the march to El Arish where Murray had decided to draw his defensive line, settling into bivouac camp at Romani, making use of the ingenious wire netting road which eased movement in the sand, and domestic views of officers having picnic meals with blankets staked as protection from the wind. Byrne had a good eye for a pleasing composition and, like many others, was fascinated by the grace of the natives and the splendours of the great sites of antiquity.

Away from the slow conventional advance of the army a completely different style of war was being waged in the hinterlands of Arabia. On 5 June 1916 Sherif Hussein of Mecca proclaimed an Arab revolt against their Turkish overlords. Relieved to find such disunity in the Mohammedan world in spite of the previous Turkish declaration of 'Jihad', or Holy War, against the Entente powers, Britain decided to assist the Arabs with money and military expertise. A young intelligence officer in Cairo, Captain T. E. Lawrence, and a handful of colleagues began to experiment with guerrilla tactics to disrupt the single railway running through the Hejaz (present-day Saudi Arabia). From early 1917 Lawrence was attached as military adviser to the Arab forces and not only masterminded many of their unconventional exploits but also ensured their military and political prominence in the closing stages of the orthodox campaign led by General Allenby when the likely tensions of any postwar settlement between Jewish, Arab, French, and British interests were becoming obvious. He and several other British officers involved such as Captains F. S. Newcombe and H. Garland, explosives experts from the Royal Engineers, and Captain Raymond Goslett, organizer of the necessary supplies, were all camera enthusiasts. Their photographs were a unique record of their transformation from carefully correct khaki uniforms to the comfortable flowing robes of the desert, their growing friendship with the Arabs,

(*c*) Egypt and Palestine: native fishermen with a seining net near Romani, February 1917. Personal photograph, S. C. Byrne, Q 57800.

(*e*) Egypt and Palestine: Emir Feisal leading his forces from his base at Wejh, 3 January 1917. Personal photograph, T. E. Lawrence, Q 58863.

the emergence of Hussein's son Feisal as the accepted leader, and the mounting of their attacks.

Lawrence's own response to the camera was revealing, given the complexities of his character and his ambivalence towards himself and his achievements. He seemed most relaxed posing in Arab robes in the desert but his ambiguity was demonstrated in his attitude towards the work of an American reporter who met him in Jerusalem in the spring of 1918. It was also to affect the postwar perception of Lawrence as one of the few individual heroes of the conflict.

Lowell Thomas was American, a talented and determined journalist who came to Europe accompanied by an equally gifted cameraman, Harry Chase, in 1917. Dismissing the Western Front as too monotonous he appealed to the Department of Information and it seems likely that John Buchan suggested he should visit the Middle East. It is unclear how much he knew of Lawrence's exploits previously, but meeting him in Jerusalem he persuaded him to give an interview and pose for photographs. Chase showed him in dark and light Arab robes adopting the manner of an enigmatic, romantic hero. Thomas did not publish them immediately partly because there was an express prohibition on any photographs of Lawrence in case they might assist the Turks, but also possibly because he saw greater potential in their postwar exploitation. In 1919 with further co-operation from Lawrence, he wove Chase's film and photographs together to make a theatrical show presented with his own commentary. It was hugely successful in America and opened to similar enthusiasm at Covent

(*d*) Egypt and Palestine: Colonel T. E. Lawrence, photographed as an enigmatic romantic in early 1918. Professional photograph, Harry Chase, Q 46094.

Garden on 14 August 1919. Entitled *With Allenby in Palestine* it emphasized Lawrence's role as 'the uncrowned king of Arabia'. It was sensationalist, colourful, and, unlike the usual run of war material, firmly centred on its leading personalities. Astonishingly popular in Britain, it went on to tour the world. Eventually it was estimated that some four million people had seen it. Combined with the conspicuous role of Lawrence as spokesman for the Arab cause at the Versailles peace conference and his growing reputation as a writer, the popularity of Lowell Thomas' enterprise inevitably contributed to the growth of the legendary persona 'Lawrence of Arabia'. But when Lawrence subsequently rejected status and fame and attempted to lose himself in the ranks of the Tank Corps and the Royal Air Force in the twenties and thirties, he repudiated any associations, such as his co-operation with Thomas, which had contributed to it. His rejection was characteristic; he had not been averse to seeing himself as the mystically pure warrior of Chase's photographs; but prone to fits of self-disgust and self-immolation, disavowed both the image and its implications. Nevertheless the popular conception was fixed and is now part of the iconography of the First World War.

In March 1917 General Murray's advance across the desert checked at Gaza, the gateway to Palestine. Two attempts to take it were bungled and Murray was recalled in disgrace. But before he left he had, apparently on his own initiative, and possibly with a view to sustaining his pleas for more troops by more publicity, arranged for a photographer to be attached to his staff. Although the appointment was made without any consultation with London, the photographs were, in the absence of any alternative, recognized as official and published as such. The only problem arising from this unorthodox manoeuvre was that after the war the photographer was forced to engage the authorities in prolonged negotiation, staking his claim for pay on a par with the photographers on the Western Front.

George Westmoreland was a professional who had previously run his own business and was serving in the ranks of the Queen's (Royal West Surrey) Regiment. He was promoted from private to sergeant on 16 December 1916 and instructed to take photographs for publicity purposes. However, he seems to have done relatively little in Murray's final months and did not start regular work until the arrival of the new commander, General Sir Edmund Allenby, in July 1917. A formidable personality and bold leader, Allenby was determined to conquer Palestine, force a defeat, and if possible drive Turkey out of the war altogether. He took Gaza in November and reached Jerusalem by 9 December, but was deterred by an unusually wet winter and the call for troops for the Western Front from continuing the offensive until late summer 1918. His cavalry played a brilliant role in his final major battle of Megiddo in September 1918 and he swept on into Syria against an enemy in increasing disarray, occupying Damascus, Beirut, and Aleppo, before news came of the Turkish armistice arranged on 30 October.

(*f*) One of the widely published photographs of General Allenby's formal entry on foot to Jerusalem on 11 December 1917. British official, George Westmoreland, Q 12616.

The successful capture of Jerusalem was virtually the only good news of 1917. Although they arrived in Britain nearly six weeks later, Westmoreland's pictures received wide publication. Much was made of the modesty of Allenby's entry on foot in contrast to that of the Kaiser during a visit in 1898; *The Illustrated London News* on 19 January 1918 wrote:

> There was no great pageantry or display of the pomp and circumstance of a victorious army.... The simplicity and reverence of his entry, on foot ... contrasts with the Kaiser's bombastic display ... arrayed like a Crusader as seen in pantomime.

But the published photographs inadvertently demonstrated some of George Westmoreland's recurring difficulties. He wrote later:

> Owing to the irregularity of my position and the rank I held, I had to exercise a great deal of tact and personality to make up for the

(*g*) Egypt and Palestine: a line of transport camels picketed on the skyline, typical of Westmoreland's preferred style and useful to the illustrated press. British official, George Westmoreland, Q 12513.

lack of prestige which the regular position carries when among superior officers with whom I was continually in contact.[1]

He had not in fact been able to get close to the hero of the hour, so was not in a good position to take very striking photographs. The mobility of the actual fighting also caused him problems; there was no settled front line and although he could and did show impressive quantities of captured guns and prisoners, there was little sense of confrontation. Given the time needed for the transmission of photographs, the illustrated press frequently resorted to the use of 'stock shots', older material which could be re-captioned to make it relevant or to artistic drawings done with a fairly liberal addition of imagination. Professional press men continued to operate but although they were comparatively unrestricted seem to have been few in number, deterred by the expense and the obstacles in communication.

The paucity of supply was shown by the repeated use of Westmoreland's work and the way in which his photographs were frequently published in several magazines simultaneously. For example, his

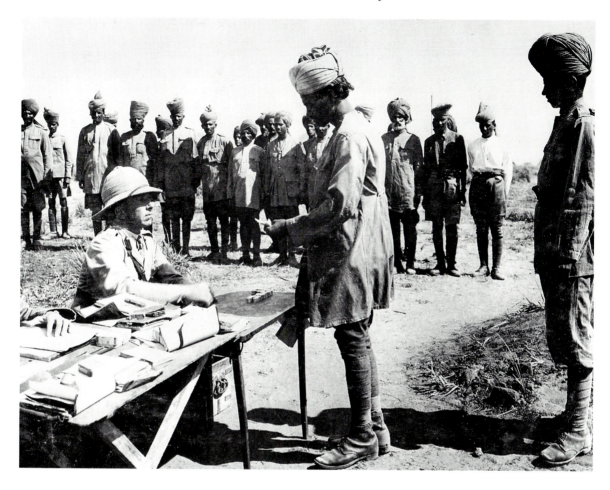

photograph of a line of camels of the Transport Corps picketed on the skyline appeared on 14 September 1918 in both *The Illustrated London News* and *The War Illustrated*. Westmoreland was at his best when he could seek out the picturesque in scenic or human terms: the Indian troops smartly turned out on parade or relaxing off-duty, the various colourful auxiliaries such as the Egyptian Labour Corps, and the beauty of the biblical landscape and the ancient sites captured. He was not the only official photographer; Frank Hurley arrived from the Western Front at the beginning of 1918 and with a small staff of two set about taking publicity pictures and making a record of the Australians involved. A good deal of Hurley's time was taken up with organizing filming and he carried out some experiments in colour photography.[2] In the event little seems to have appeared in the contemporary British press probably because of difficulties of dispatch, its subordination to more general coverage, and its administration by the Australian War Records Section in London, consistently more concerned for the long-term record than publicity.

The record of the war in Egypt and Palestine was largely composed

(*h*) Egypt and Palestine: a routine procedure, a pay parade of troops of the 7th Indian Division. British official, George Westmoreland, Q 12499.

of private and official photographs, though in comparison with other theatres the number of official photographs was small. This was probably due to the uncertainty surrounding Westmoreland's appointment and the lack of direct interest in his role. On more than one occasion he was forced to dip into his own pocket to pay for the necessary materials and not unnaturally this may have discouraged him. Initially the press seems to have afforded quite a number of professionals in Egypt but as the campaign first slackened and then halted in 1916 it seems to have doubted the wisdom of expenditure and even when it regained momentum to have relied largely on official photographs if they were available and stock shots or drawings if they were not. The published account of the war, like the private and official photographs, offered an attractive series of vignettes rather than a narrative of the campaign; the pattern was, with minor variations, repeated in the other theatre of war against Turkey, Mesopotamia.

Mesopotamia

In October 1914 Britain dispatched a force from India to guard the oilfields at the head of the Persian Gulf and to profit if possible from the general Arab unrest in the Turkish provinces. Technically Turkey had not yet declared war and the Indian Expeditionary Force waited until after 1 November before establishing its headquarters at Basra. Then as in Egypt, the commander, Lieutenant-General Sir Arthur Barrett, was tempted to gain some room for manoeuvre by advancing further inland along the great rivers, the Tigris and the Euphrates. He took his orders not from the War Cabinet in London but from the commander-in-chief in India which further clouded the already opaque strategic thinking behind the expedition. Its pretext was slight and the climate given to extremes of heat, cold, and wet. The rivers offered the only practical means of transport in a barren country where disease was rampant. The distances from the War Cabinet in London and the commander in Delhi were so great and the lines of communication so long that control of information was not an important issue. A few intrepid press photographers and correspondents with cameras seem to have made occasional visits but as there was relatively little happening for long periods they confined themselves to general material about the country, the frequent floods, and the problems of transport. However, private cameras were common and used freely. In the absence of any official photography until the second half of the war, and the difficulties it posed for the ordinary professional, some of its most interesting aspects were only recorded by amateurs, in particular the longest and most humiliating siege in British history, the 147 day siege of Kut which lasted from 7 December 1915 until the surrender of 29 April 1916.

(*i*) Mesopotamia: a wry presentation by the professional press of the difficulties of accommodation and transport in the natural hazards of the country. *The Sphere*, 20 May 1916.

To the new ambitious commander, General Sir John Nixon, and his superiors, the city of Baghdad beckoned as a possible prize and potential means of inflicting a blow to Turkish pride even if it was about 500

ONE OF THE HUMOURS OF CAMPAIGNING IN THE DESERT—AN OFFICER'S CAMP FLOODED OUT

During the flood season in Mesopotamia wash-outs are of frequent occurrence. The country is one of extremes—the weather is seldom moderate, either the country is baking in the sun or it is deluged by waterspouts and floods. Accompanying the floods high winds are often experienced, which heap up the water and send it over the river and canal banks, to the intense discomfort of such troops as are unhappily quartered near the centre of the disturbance

BRITISH TROOPS DOUBLING ACROSS A PONTOON BRIDGE BUILT OVER THE MARSHY BED OF A RIVER

miles from the main base at Basra. An expedition was mounted in late 1915. The 6th Indian Division led by Major-General Sir Charles Townshend advanced successfully but was routed twenty-three miles from Baghdad at the battle of Ctesiphon on 22–4 November. Townshend's headlong retreat took him over 200 miles back to the unappealing village of Kut situated on a loop of the river Tigris where he and his men were trapped.

Three men apparently had cameras with them during the siege, Major A. S. Cane of the Royal Army Medical Corps, Major P. C. Saunders of the Supply and Transport Corps, and the Reverend Harold Spooner, the Church of England padre. Their collections showed, as professionals rarely had the opportunity to do, their own army in retreat and included the long columns of horsemen riding in clouds of dust, the heavy artillery being dragged along, the masses of wooden transport carts laden with supplies or prisoners and casualties too badly wounded to walk, and the hurried halts for food and water. In Kut itself there was rash optimism and a blithe disregard for any realistic organization of supplies. The strength and persistence of the Turkish army had been seriously underestimated and it successfully blocked all relief attempts.

The photographs showed the details of daily life; the Arab traders whose stores were rapidly depleted, the unfortunate Turkish prisoners, the line of continuously manned trench defences, and the ingenious improvised weapons such as an anti-aircraft gun mounted on a large cask and a trench mortar made out of an aircraft engine cylinder. As the siege lengthened and the weather turned cold and wet, food supplies diminished, diseases multiplied, and medicines ran out. Some 4,000 of the original garrison strength of 17,000 were casualties. Major Saunders took photographs of the makeshift hospitals, and in a diary addressed to his family, one of the occupants, Lieutenant L. S. Bell Syer, described the officers' ward (*plate k*):

> You would probably have the shock of your life if you could only see the place I am in. It is just an ordinary Arab house, my bed being under a kind of ledge in the interior or courtyard. This ledge is all the roof we have, the courtyard being absolutely open to the rain and wind. There are four beds in the niche under this ledge so close together that there is barely room to get between, mine is one of these. In the centre of the courtyard is a drain down which all the filth of the household has been poured for many years, in another corner of the yard the hospital orderlies cook their food over a wood fire. What would an English civilian doctor say to this? I leave the Tommies' hospital for your own imagination to draw upon, as also the Sepoys' who have not even got beds.[3]

In fact the photographs need to be studied in conjunction with the written records for their full significance to be appreciated. They do not portray in sensationalist terms the privations suffered by the garrison in Kut. That was done later by the press photographs of some

(*j*) The siege of Kut: a wounded Turk being transported on one of the ubiquitous wooden carts during the retreat to Kut, November 1915. Personal photograph, P. C. Saunders, HU 51375.

(*k*) The siege of Kut: the British officers' hospital in January 1916 with Lieutenant L. S. Bell Syer's bed on the extreme right. Personal photograph, P. C. Saunders, HU 51390.

of the survivors released from Turkish prisons which showed their emaciated bodies and strained faces. What the private photographs did indicate was the sustained correct bearing and continued respect for military discipline of all concerned. By means of stock photographs of the ancient sites such as Ctesiphon, supplemented by the meagre work of the few press photographers with the relief force, plus maps and graphic representations, the British press had run regular features on the 21-week siege usually with the rider that it was only a matter of time until it was lifted. The eventual surrender was a disaster for British prestige and another triumph for Turkey, the recent victor at Gallipoli.

In mid-1916 control of events in Mesopotamia was taken out of the hands of the Indian commander-in-chief in Delhi and passed to London. Under the command of a gifted and popular general, Stanley Maude, some of the worst deficiencies of the administrative machine were made good and preparations were made for another assault on Baghdad to begin in December. As ever rain, heat, and disease impeded progress and the Turks fought courageously but Maude was able to enter the city on 11 March 1917. Despite various notions drawn on maps in London for linking the two campaigns against Turkey in Palestine and Mesopotamia, nothing ever came of them and although skirmishes north of Baghdad continued, the main thrust halted until just before the end of the war when a final brisk move secured the oilfields at Mosul.

It may have been at Maude's instigation or possibly the result of

(*l*) The siege of Kut: one of the press photographs of survivors showing an emaciated Indian soldier who had also endured some months in the notoriously bad conditions of a Turkish prison before being exchanged. Professional press photograph, Q 79446.

requests from London but in early 1917 the High Command asked that photographs of 'sufficient interest' taken by members of the forces should, with the consent of their owners be duplicated for circulation as publicity material. Copies were sent to the War Office and to Army Headquarters in India as well as being kept locally. In this way a useful quantity of material built up. But the time-lag between gathering it, dispatching it, and its circulation from the War Office to the press not unnaturally inhibited its publication. However, by this time the

(*m*) Mesopotamia: cinematic style photographs of 'types' in Baghdad 1917: a straw carrier. British official, Ariel Varges, Q 24471.

(*n*) Mesopotamia: 'types' in Baghdad: a water coolie. British official, Ariel Varges, Q 24480.

(*o*) Mesopotamia; a Kurd carrying the body of his child, dead from starvation in the dislocation of the final breakdown of the Ottoman empire, to the Moslem cemetery in Kirkuk. British official, Ariel Varges, Q 24728.

Department of Information was anxious to obtain some official photographs. An American ciné and still photographer, Ariel Varges, had been working in Salonika for one of his country's large news organizations, the International Film Service. Nothing momentous was happening there and so when asked to transfer by the Department of Information and the War Office Cinematograph Committee, the body chiefly concerned with the organization of official film, he agreed. He was in time to cover Maude's entry into Baghdad but with the subsequent dearth of action he spent a good deal of time in the streets of the city taking pictures of 'types', old men, spruce merchants, coolies bent under their loads, and women veiled and unveiled with their robes

fluttering about them. Possibly because of his cinematic experience the photographs have the sense, rare amongst those of the First World War, of spontaneous action only momentarily arrested.

On 18 November 1917 General Maude died of the cholera endemic in the city. His funeral and military ceremonial were recorded by Varges but it was four months before the pictures appeared in the English press. Left very much to his own devices, in early 1918 he visited Kut which had been retaken the previous February, and took photographs of the careful maintenance of the military cemeteries and the various memorials, as well as of the story-tellers in the bazaar 'telling the tale of the siege'. They were used, again about four months later, in *The War Illustrated* on 29 June to make a general page of pictures under the heading 'Faring Beyond Babylon Under The British Flag'. It also seems likely that Varges, looking for excitement, accompanied the 'Dunsterville force', a group of officers commanded by Major-General L. C. Dunsterville who set off with more initiative than resources to attempt to stake the claim of British interests in the Caspian area.

The laborious delay in transmission led not surprisingly to a certain amount of mild misrepresentation and repetition in an illustrated press short of material. Varges took some excellent pictures of prisoners

(*p*) Mesopotamia: Turkish prisoners captured at the battle of Ramadie under escort in September 1917. Published twice in 1918, first as part of a general feature and later as showing a current event when Turkey finally surrendered. British official, Ariel Varges, Q 24294.

captured at the Battle of Ramaidi, one of the actions fought north of Baghdad in September 1917. The Turks had an appalling reputation for their treatment of captives borne out by the experiences of those taken after the siege of Kut. Varges' photographs, although four months old even when first published in *The War Illustrated* of 9 February 1918, were used in a manner more than a little superior as the headline read 'From the Field of Conflict to the Camp of Care' and went on to point out the benefit of baths, boots, and proper bureaucracy which followed capture by the British. At least one of the same photographs was used by *The Illustrated London News* on 9 November after the final surrender of Turkey on 30 October 1918 with the implication that these were recently 'Defeated [prisoners]: Turks surrendering and on the way to internment'. The aftermath of war was already clear in the general breakdown of law and order, and famine and disease were rife. Some of Varges' final and most touching photographs taken in late 1918 showed the stream of refugees looking for help and the common incidence of death from starvation in the areas north and east of Baghdad. It seems unlikely that any of these were published, overshadowed as they were by the end of the campaign in Europe.

Throughout the war photography for publication of the Mesopotamian campaign was a series of makeshifts. The difficulties of transport and communication combined with the long periods of little interest deterred the professional, the assembly of private photographs was ineffectual, and the only official photographer of the British effort was a late arrival and a foreigner. The catastrophes of muddle and military incompetence were exposed by the written word rather than by visual evidence in the findings of the various government commissions set up during the war. Press coverage was constant in its perception of the campaign as remote, exotic, and prone to disaster both natural and military. This was exacerbated by the fact that most of its troops were drawn from the Empire in India and so although nods were made in the direction of sacrifice in a common cause, the appalling hardships remained a very distant problem.

The peripheral nature of the campaigns in Egypt, Palestine, and Mesopotamia meant that they were unlikely ever to receive the kind of concerted lobbying of interested parties that went into the appointment of official photographers on the Western Front, nor were Varges and Westmoreland subject to the constraints of a large, static military hierarchy. Neither of their appointments was orthodox, Westmoreland being summoned by a personal military initiative and Varges, an American, being asked to work for the British government because he happened to be available. In the event a surprising number of their pictures were published showing the strength of demand despite the problems of transmission. However, on the whole, their picturesque qualities may have contributed to the estimation of the war against Turkey as being of secondary importance. It did not have a similar recurrent imagery of struggle as did the conflict in the trenches on the Western Front. The exception to the run of generally anonymous participants was the image and fame of T.E. Lawrence but this was achieved after the war and brought about not only by his own abilities but widely publicized by Lowell Thomas. However, from Egypt, Palestine, and Mesopotamia, the quantity of personal photographs which survives offers evidence, in some cases extraordinary, of individual experience, and together with the work of the official photographers provides some of the most interesting if not the most belligerent accounts of the war.

5

TRADITIONAL SILENCE:
The war at sea

> The attitude of the Navy towards publicity was very slow to change, and I think I can say today with a perfectly clear mind, that though the officers of the Navy may grudgingly agree that some measure of publicity is an absolute necessity, since the Fleet belongs to the nation (i.e. the public) and not to the Navy, they thoroughly detest it. The lower deck, perhaps, regards the matter somewhat more jocularly.[1]

So wrote the former Chief Naval Censor, Rear-Admiral Sir Douglas Brownrigg, in his memoirs published shortly after the war. Recalled from retirement in 1914 he took charge of the organization of naval censorship. At the outbreak of war his office was attached to the Press Bureau but easily dominated it. Brownrigg's own long service gave him the advantage of personal friendship and knowledge of the highest echelons of the formidable naval hierarchy, as well as consciousness of its ingrained tradition of aloof secrecy. His was a difficult role of reconciling opposing contradictions; his service's dislike of publicity and its practitioners, and the vociferous demands of the press and propaganda organizations for access and material. On the whole he personally favoured release of information, even bad news, provided it was reported soberly and without sensationalism, but at the same time he sympathized with his service about the disruption and inconvenience of dealing with the press. On board ship a supernumerary such as a photographer seemed to many an impertinence when space and resources for fighting men were at a premium.

Brownrigg's memoirs describe his struggle in finding acceptance for official reporting and his particular problems with film and photography:

> The attitude of the fleet towards photographers, both 'still' and 'moving' was curious. It invariably tried to prevent them being sent up, saying that there were plenty of men in the fleet capable of doing all that was required. Every artifice and stratagem down to downright lying and misuse of high officials' names had to be put in use to succeed in planting my professional photographers and cinematographers on the fleet on these occasions....[2]

The upshot was that although the navy eventually came to tolerate

official professional photographers it was on a far more limited basis than the army. With the brief exception of the Gallipoli expedition in 1915 when it had first claim on the services of Ernest Brooks, no official photographers were ever permanently attached. Professionals were allowed access to sea and shore operations by a system of permits valid for one assignment at a time. As a result the official record would be slight in comparison with the army and although photography by sailors was to a certain extent encouraged, it was bound to be fairly haphazard. In any case, for both professional and amateur, war at sea and the complexities of its supporting organization on land were to prove particularly difficult to photograph comprehensively.

However, the navy had long-standing relationships with professional photographic firms at its various bases and with studios specializing in portraiture on whom it relied for its own needs and whose material was a regular staple of press supply. These continued albeit restricted by the need to observe the censorship, and together

(a) A practice salvo from HMS *Royal Sovereign*. British official, Q 17991.

(b) Artistic coverage of the Battle of Jutland: a drawing by Arthur J. W. Burgess of 'A German battleship disabled by British gunfire'. *The Sphere*, 24 June 1916.

(c) The strength of the Royal Navy as shown in *The Illustrated London News*, 18 July 1914. Professional photographs by Cribb.

THE BATTLE OF JUTLAND : *A GERMAN BATTLESHIP DISABLED BY BRITISH GUNFIRE.*

DRAWN BY ARTHUR J. W. BURGESS, 1916

TEETH OF THE NAVY: GUNS THE KING WILL SEE AT SPITHEAD.

PHOTOGRAPHS BY CRIBB, SOUTHSEA.

A VESSEL AND ARMAMENT OF THE TYPE WHICH SIR PERCY SCOTT CONSIDERS HAVE BEEN RENDERED OF LITTLE AVAIL BY THE SUBMARINE AND THE TORPEDO: THE "DREADNOUGHT" FIRING HER AFT TURRET GUNS.

THE MAN BEHIND THE GUN STILL AN INDISPENSABLE FACTOR IN THE SCIENCE OF NAVAL WARFARE: GUNNERY ON BOARD A DESTROYER— THE DEFLECTION-TEACHER AND ITS MAZE OF WHEELS.

(d) Taken from HMS *Invincible*: HMS *Inflexible* picking up survivors from the *Gneisenau* sunk during the battle of the Falkland Islands, 8 December 1914. Personal photograph, A. Duckworth, Q 20896.

with whatever amateur work was offered formed the bulk of photographs available for publication at the outbreak of war and for some time after. In August 1914 it was confidently expected that victory would be won by the largest and most heavily gunned navy in the world after a major encounter of capital ships. After all it had been Admiralty policy for the preceding decades that the Royal Navy should aim to be twice the size of any two potential enemies. British influence prevailed as her ships cruised the sea-lanes of her worldwide empire and protected her routes of commerce. This confidence was reflected in the illustrated press as the prospect of war drew nearer; a major review of the fleet took place at Spithead on 18–20 July and as usual not only the major agencies such as Central News and Alfieri but the photographic firms in Portsmouth such as Cribb, Symonds, and Wright and Logan made it their business to cover it. *The Illustrated London News* of 18 July drew heavily on their work to make up a photographic portfolio of the occasion. It described the line of twenty-four big-gun battleships, the dreadnoughts, as 'England's floating ramparts' and their guns as 'the teeth of the Navy' and went on in a feature headed 'War and Peace' to illustrate life on board and its mixture of domesticity, regular worship, and training for conflict (*plate c*).

However, the much-vaunted decisive victory did not come although the first months of war saw several brisk encounters: at Heligoland Bight in the North Sea on 28 August where a dramatic chase failed

to catch the German High Seas Fleet, at Coronel off Chile on 1 November where an elderly British battle squadron was defeated, and at the Falkland Islands on 8 December where, in revenge for previous humiliation, all but one of a German squadron of five cruisers was sunk. For obvious reasons the only cameras to record these actions were private and as with material from the Western Front the press was prepared to pay liberally for the opportunity to publish, but in view of the inevitable delay would juxtapose its first reports with whatever naval photographs were immediately to hand. News of victory in the battle of the Falkland Islands arrived well before any photographs and the early accounts made use of some recent pictures, taken mostly by serving officers, of the fleet in the North Sea. *The War Illustrated* on 9 January was typical in setting the first report besides a spread which included a selection of these, headlined 'Jellicoe and his Fleet in readiness for "Der Tag"'. These included the Admiral 'on the qui vive' climbing up to the forebridge of his flagship the *Iron Duke*, views of rough seas setting decks awash and ships steaming in line ahead. The photograph of Jellicoe was in fact one of the very few ever taken of him at sea during his period as commander-in-chief (*plate f*). He was a naturally reticent man who, like many of his officers, shunned personal and general publicity.

   When some of the private material taken in the Falklands became available it demonstrated the problem of recording naval action; it all

(*e*) The battle of Jutland recorded by a private camera: the final moments of HMS *Invincible* seen from HMS *Benbow*, 31 May 1916. Personal photograph, anon., SP 2470.

(f) One of the few photographs of Admiral Sir John Jellicoe in his role as Commander-in-Chief of the Grand Fleet, released to the press in December 1914. Personal photograph, F. Rees, Q 55499.

(g) Admiral Sir David Beatty, posing deliberately for the camera with his hat at its famous 'Beatty tilt' shortly after his appointment as Commander-in-Chief. British official, Ernest Brooks, Q 19571.

happened at a distance. The big guns could fire over a range of thirteen miles and encounters with the enemy might mean simply the sighting of a smudge on the horizon. Use of smoke for concealment, the speed of ships steaming flat out at 'action stations', and the vital role of every man on duty, meant, to say the least, limited opportunities for photography. Often only when the heat of the action was over and in a brisk but customary change of role the victor turned rescuer could photographs, similar to those of the survivors of the *Gneisenau* struggling in the water towards HMS *Invincible*, be taken. This was to be true of photographs of all the major naval engagements – only a few taken usually after the main action by amateurs survive. They might

(*h*) Experiments in naval aviation: the remains of the Sopwith Pup in which Squadron Commander E. Dunning met his death after attempting a deck landing on board HMS *Furious* being hauled out of the sea. Personal photograph, Wilfred Dyke Acland, Q 96522.

(*i*) Relaxation on board ship: officers playing hockey on the quarterdeck of a battleship *c.* 1917. British official, Q 18043.

(*j*) Stokers busy shovelling coal into the enormous boilers of a battleship, 1917. British official, Q 18593.

(*k*) Women in shipbuilding: women being instructed in the 'comparatively simple work' of assembly of small parts for the electrical equipment of ships at the Royal Naval Dockyard, Portsmouth. Admiralty Shipyard Labour Department, HU 51900.

(*l*) Women's Royal Naval Service recruits in various garb at unaccustomed squad drill, published as an aid for recruitment in *The War Illustrated*, 13 April 1918. British official, G. P. Lewis, Q 18695.

or might not be released to the press at the time according to the desire of the taker, the interest of his commander, and possibility of communication with the Censor's office. Even in the battle which came closest to being the expected decisive encounter of capital ships, fought at Jutland in the North Sea on 31 May 1916, the accounts of it drew largely on the skills of artists to re-create the excitement and on the stock shots of the ships involved available from the professional firms. The censorship at this time seems to have been especially strict and even when the heroes and survivors reached the shore there was little opportunity for ordinary professionals. Not unexpectedly none of the private photographs which showed British ships sinking were considered suitable for contemporary publication.

The far-flung activities of the Royal Navy made amateur photography especially important as a record not only of battle and the lives of the men but also of its general development during the war. Some major technical innovations particularly in naval aviation were first recorded by private cameras. The Royal Naval Air Service was established on 23 June 1914 and quickly became proficient at a multiplicity of roles including patrol duty, reconnaissance, and some early experimental strategic bombing, which consisted simply of tossing some missile out of the aircraft by hand. However, the scope for its aircraft would obviously be greatly extended if they could be launched from and return to a mother ship. The first successful experiments in take-off and landing at sea were carried out on board HMS *Furious* in 1917. Captain Wilfred Dyke Acland took a careful sequence showing the Sopwith Pup flown by Squadron Commander E. Dunning skidding to a halt against the ropes strung along the deck. But triumph turned to disaster during a later second attempt; the aeroplane missed the primitive arrestors, and toppled off the deck. The crumpled wreck was photographed as it was salvaged from the sea (*plate h*).

Given the navy's hostility to official reporting it was ironic that technically the first official photographer was a naval appointment although in the event Ernest Brooks' photographs of Gallipoli reflected the altered balance of roles between the army and navy. But despite their successful publication, when the forces were finally evacuated and Brooks applied to Admiral Sir Douglas Brownrigg for further directions, nothing came of it; he was transferred to the Western Front and afterwards only available by special arrangement. Brownrigg sighed: 'I subsequently had to go on my hands and knees to the Minister of Information (Lord Beaverbrook) to borrow him. I have never ceased regretting our losing hold of him.'[3] For the rest of the war photographers were allowed to make excursions to the fleet or its shore bases on a single permit basis only.

However, when official photographers became accepted on the Western Front in mid-1916 Brownrigg and Ivor Nicholson of Wellington House pressed that at least one and preferably more, should be permanently attached to the Grand Fleet. They made little headway until later in the year when a change occurred at the very top. In

November Admiral Jellicoe was succeeded by the far more flamboyant Admiral Sir David Beatty. The latter did not shy from publicity and although it was still not generally welcomed far more arrangements became possible. Although no permanent appointments were made, Nicholson was able to use two agency men regularly, Robert Humphrey of Topical Press, and Charles Brown of Alfieri. Brownrigg also had what he called a succession of 'tame' photographers such as Bernard Grant of the *Daily Mirror*. In addition, Ivor Castle and Ernest Brooks were occasionally available. It was the latter who took photographs of the new commander-in-chief shortly after his appointment. These underlined the contrast with his predecessor; instead of a snatched snap Beatty posed directly to the camera, his cap set at the famous 'Beatty tilt', emphasizing his craggy good looks (*plate g*).

These introduced the large range of photographs taken in 1917. Some excellent work was done which, judging by its frequent use in the press, proved generally satisfactory in quality if not in quantity. Forced to cast around for subjects which might suggest warlike activity and general readiness for action in the peaceful conditions of fleet anchorages, the photographers took some spectacular shots of the guns firing practice salvoes (*plate a*), the drama of ships steaming in line ahead, and then turned to life on board, the exigencies of the boiler room, and the relaxation of men in their ward rooms, with their pets, or at games (*plates i, j*). Such work provided useful 'stock' shots not tied to any particular time or place. Lacking opportunity, the photographers made the most of whatever came their way by covering aspects of life above and below deck not previously considered worthy of much note.

The navy never suffered from the same desperate need of numbers as the army; instead its crisis occurred over the appalling losses of merchant shipping to submarine attack and consequent need to build ships faster than ever before. Since the uncertain outcome of the battle of Jutland Germany had concentrated on the undersea war with alarming success. Eagerly awaited supplies were sent to the bottom of the sea and shipping losses occurred at a greater rate than they could be replaced. In March and April 1917 the total losses of all Allied shipping reached the devastating totals of over 603,000 and 894,000 tonnes respectively. Although these figures were not made public it was obvious from the increased shortages and the introduction of rationing that the crisis was grave. The need of the press for material to suggest counter-attack and the growth of shipbuilding extended official and professional photography to naval industry. Stories if not statistics of the work being carried out were legion and often combined with rebuttals of the enemy's prowess. *The Illustrated London News* of 19 January 1918 was typical; some striking photographs of submarine construction were accompanied by the following:

Stories of big craft of extraordinary dimensions of 'frightfulness' appear every other week in some of the press, mostly by way of

(*m*) A British submarine under construction appears as a mysterious geometric pattern of circular steel girders, published in *The Illustrated London News*, 19 January 1918. British official, Q 18524.

quotation from Amsterdam and Copenhagen journals on the strength of accounts by correspondents at Kiel and Wilhelmshaven or as related by wandering neutral commercial travellers. Mostly the yarns are palpably of the 'make your flesh creep' order bogies. On the other hand, nothing is allowed to get out of what we are doing – though, as a fact, our submarine building goes on day and night.

The urgent need for more ships of every type and the steady syphoning off of men to the battlefront led to the process known as 'substitution' whereby women were encouraged to enter industry in order to sustain production. But shipbuilding was a bastion of traditional attitudes and practices and professional photographers were commissioned to provide example and encouragement probably as much to the industry itself as for general circulation. The descriptions often conveyed a tone of mild surprise at women's capacity. The Admiralty Shipyard Labour Department compiled a substantial portfolio, 'for the purpose of demonstrating the work which could be undertaken by women to increase production and to release men for service with the colours'.[4] Pictures were taken on a national basis in the premises of commercial firms and naval dockyards showing women involved as shipwrights, platers, riveters, and blacksmiths in the heavy work of shipbuilding, and acquiring the precision skills of sawing, milling, grinding, and fitting required for marine engineering. Women working in the electrical shop of the Royal Naval Dockyard at Portsmouth were captioned as:

> Women under instruction in assembling components for electrical switches in warships. This was comparatively simple work which requires intelligence and a light touch. This was work for which women under suitable supervision excelled. (*plate k*)

and another one read:

> Work of this kind was well within the capacity of women, and the number here employed suggests that the head of the Department has been both enthusiastic and successful in training them and arranging their work, in order to meet the demand for increased output from the dockyard.[5]

The formation in November 1917 of the Women's Royal Naval Service attracted the attention of the press and official photographers. Commanded by the formidable Mrs Katherine Furse (later Dame) it quickly established its reputation for demanding a high quality of recruit and submitting her to a rigorous training. By early 1918 two official photographers were working full time on the home front for the Ministry of Information and one of these, G. P. Lewis,[6] was commissioned to produce a comprehensive set of pictures with a view to publication, as an aid to recruitment and also with a nod in the direction of the permanent record. The recently founded Imperial War Museum was casting about for material and had a particularly active

(*n*) The WRNS: a study accentuating femininity in the office-holder and her surroundings, Miss Edith Crowdy, Deputy Director of the Women's Royal Naval Service, 1918. British official, G. P. Lewis, Q 19695.

Women's Work Committee which had realized that photographs would be an essential part of its record of women's role. The committee arranged that it should share the services of Lewis with the Ministry. His photographs showed the new recruits in an array of assorted garments at unaccustomed squad drill at Crystal Palace, the founder members of the organization in their offices, and the different jobs of clerks, telephonists, sailmakers, cooks, waitresses, and motor-drivers being learnt and practised at the various naval bases. He made attractive studies of their living accommodation in dormitories and their relaxation areas. Overall it was a reassuring image of femininity, industry, and propriety and was used as such in the press; for example on 13 April 1918 *The War Illustrated* published a selection which was in effect an appeal for recruits and said:

> The Wrens must come forward with a serious wish to help their country to win the war, and with the determination to win the best possible reputation for women's service in war time. The work, it is frankly explained, is strenuous, but it is hoped that the conditions maintained will be such as to ensure the health and content of all who join. (*plate l*)

On the night of 22–3 April 1918 the Royal Navy undertook an exploit which had all the qualities of audaciousness and excitement that its main roles as convoy escort and blockade enforcer in the second half of the war had lacked; a raid designed to deny to the Germans use of the U-boat bases at Zeebrugge and Ostend. Though

(*p*) The photograph released four years later; survivors from HMS *Audacious* being picked up off the Ulster coast, 27 October 1914. Probably private origin, Q 47967.

the victory was more apparent than real, as the plan was only partially successful then and in its second attempt at Ostend on 9–10 May, the morale effect was enormous. Coming as it did just after the calamities of the German spring offensive on the Western Front, it gave a badly needed fillip to the battered confidence of the nation and its allies. For once photographs, if not of the action itself, but at least showing the triumphant, battle-worn ships and their crews, were plentiful. Even the Admiralty communiqué broke into colourful expression:

> *Vindictive* was fitted along the port side with a high false deck, whence ran the 18 brows, or gangways, by which the storming and demolition parties were to land. . . . The gangways were lowered and scraped and rebounded upon the high parapet of the Mole as *Vindictive* rolled. . . . The men were magnificent. Every officer bears the same testimony. The mere landing on the Mole was a perilous business; it involved a passage across the crashing, splintering gangways, a drop over the parapet into the field of fire of the German machine-guns which swept its length, and a further drop of some 16ft to the surface of the Mole itself. Many were killed and more were wounded as they crowded up to the gangways; but nothing hindered the orderly and speedy landing by every gangway.[7]

The Illustrated London News of 4 May gave what was possibly the largest picture spread devoted to a single operation during the war; it filled twenty-one pages with photographs and graphic representation of the news and emphasized that this stirring exploit had taken place appropriately on St George's day. Other illustrated publications followed similar lines. However, the quantity of photographs available owed little to official commission but rather to the fact that press and

(*o*) The celebrated Zeebrugge raid: a page showing the battered *Vindictive* and her triumphant crew from a 21-page feature using professional photographs. *The Illustrated London News*, 4 May 1918.

agency photographers were permitted access to the shore bases. The navy remained implacable to the end.

As its Chief Censor lamented at regular intervals throughout the war, naval dislike of the apparently vulgar press went deep and, combined with the ease with which it could evade tiresome demands by simply sailing away, meant that it made few concessions. In some ways it undermined its own role by refusing to admit some of its disasters even when they had become an open secret. The loss of the battleship *Audacious* sunk by a mine off Ulster on 27 October 1914 was concealed on the direct orders of the commander-in-chief. Photographs of the rescue of her crew were taken but not published until four years after the event. Although rumour was rife, not until after the armistice was the loss officially admitted. It was Brownrigg's longest disagreement with his superiors as not only had he been in favour of a statement at the time but, as the loss became a certainty and severely undermined the credibility of official information, thought that the risk of recrimination was worth the truth of disclosure. The irony of official naval photography was that throughout the war its Chief Censor was concerned to arrange for more rather than less. Although his suppression of the finer points of technical detail such as wireless masts and gunnery was strict, he nevertheless made a substantial effort to secure publicity for the navy. Despite the succession of the extrovert Beatty to the reticent Jellicoe as commander-in-chief to the Grand Fleet, his task was not made any easier by the change in the role of the service from its prewar expectations of decisive war winner in spectacular action to the equally important but decidedly less glamorous blockade enforcer and convoy escort. There were fewer obvious occasions to publicize and a disinclination to admit to such drudgery. Its own and the public's reaction to the news of Zeebrugge showed how little changed were the basic assumptions about the role of the Royal Navy. In photographic terms the prevailing attitudes meant that the service allowed no coherent or sustained attempt to publicize or document its role during the war; where photographs exist of major action at sea they virtually all come from private cameras, as do those of the more remote bases and operations. Professional photographers operating on an official permit basis were able to build up only 'stock' shots showing routine scenes and incidents and not a narrative of events. However, forced to seek maximum material in the limited time available at sea, they began to widen their photographic range and to produce what might be called documentary work. Ashore it was the entry of women into the shipbuilding industry and the navy itself which attracted the most photographic attention, but the initiative was on the whole left either to the press or the propaganda organization. But once the war was over and the Imperial War Museum was actively collecting, the Admiralty was naturally eager to see its contribution recognized. On 9 May 1919 it circulated an order[8] asking for photographs of 'ships, actions, damages or incidents of interest' taken by officers and men to be lent to the Museum and that 'utmost publicity should be given to this matter'. Publicity in wartime appeared to many as boastful and dangerous advertisement but their proper share of the national record was quite another matter. The response was excellent.

6

A NEW PARTICIPANT:
The civilian at war

Although the First World War changed the basic organization of the nation the transformation took place gradually. For much of the first two years life went on very much as before. There was no doubt about the extent of support for the cause as volunteers came in droves. It was therefore natural that the official propaganda organization at Wellington House should concentrate its first efforts on cultivation of allied and neutral countries and not seriously consider the civilians at home until the second half of the war. Then the need for manpower for front and factory and the depressing effects of shortages brought about by the U-boat campaign caused concern for civilian morale and willingness to continue the fight, and the official propaganda organization extended its remit. However, through the operations of the Press Bureau in relation to the home press and the multiplicity of official, semi-official, and officially backed voluntary organizations concerned with recruiting to the forces and the auxiliary organizations, the civilian was subject to a modicum of official interest right from the outbreak of war. This would affect photographers chiefly through the censorship and what was or was not permissible to publish. Initially, severe prohibitions on unauthorized photography of all subjects remotely military or industrial were enforced but as the struggle engulfed more people and resources, the rules were applied less strictly and, eventually, encouragement given to official as well as press photography on the home front.

To begin with the press assumed that as in previous struggles there would be a clear-cut division between the military and the civilian and in their reporting concentrated on the enthusiasm and patriotism underpinning the mobilization and training for war. The enormous influx of volunteers to the armed forces was recorded in scenes of queues outside recruiting offices all over the country. After four days of war *The Sphere* of 8 August had a generous spread showing touching family farewells, reservists seeking transport to their depots, ammunition being taken by wagon from the arsenal near the Serpentine, an aeroplane propeller stuffed on to a lorry with the ingenuous caption, 'What they [aeroplanes] are capable of doing against the huge Zeppelin airships and foreign aeroplanes is hardly known yet.' Given the difficulties of obtaining photographs from the Western Front, the training of the forces at home was an obvious possibility for the illustrated press

(*a*) Industry: a woman glassworker with a tube of rolled glass in Lancashire. British official, G. P. Lewis, Q 28392.

120

(*b*) Outbreak of war, August 1914: a queue of volunteers for enlistment outside a recruiting office in Whitehall. This kind of scene was repeated in the press for months. Professional press photograph, Q 42033.

(*c*) The army in training: the 2/14th London Scottish Regiment cheerfully practise a bayonet charge, June 1915. Professional press photograph, Q 53753.

(*d*) Belgian refugees; two Belgian women with their collecting boxes at Newmarket racecourse in October 1914. Note the Boy Scouts on duty to guarantee probity. Professional press photograph, Q 53361.

(*e*) Christmas cheer 1914; a soldier and his girlfriends sledging at Epsom published in the *Daily Mirror*, 25 January 1915. Professional press photograph, Q 53560.

(*f*) The comfort for prisoners which attracted criticism; a room at Donnington Hall. Central Prisoner of War Committee photograph, Q 65498.

but was only allowed on a permit basis. These were issued in response to request and usually allowed access to a military or industrial site for a single occasion. To begin with, the fear of inadvertently releasing useful information to the enemy was such that press photographers going about their assignments even with the proper papers could find themselves under suspicion. However, persistence ensured regular features showing items such as the army practising bayonet charges in Richmond Park, the Royal Naval Division drilling at Crystal Palace, and the auxiliary organizations such as the Boy Scouts busy with countless extra check duties in connection with wartime rules and regulations.

On 14 November 1914 *The Sphere* did something rare in the use of photographs; it took fourteen and spread them across two pages headed: 'The Recruit – How He is Trained through the Early Stages of a Soldier's Career' and showed all the different phases from the moment of arriving at the recruiting tent at Horse Guards' Parade, swearing the oath of allegiance, marching off to the depot, lessons in wearing puttees, shooting, drilling, and fitness exercises to the smart final parade. The photographs were general in content rather than the story of an individual but nevertheless the presentation was a much closer relationship of words and pictures than usual.

(*g*) The shock of the German bombardment of east coast towns in December 1914: the cover of *The Sphere* neatly combines outrage at the hurt to civilians, women, and the church in an artistic drawing of an incident outside the Baptist chapel in Hartlepool. *The Sphere*, 26 December 1914.

As the war went on and large contingents of troops arrived from the Empire, their activities offered further scope. Events such as the first Anzac Day memorial parade to the service in Westminster Abbey on 25 April 1916 combined the spectacular with the patriotic and

THE SPHERE

AN ILLUSTRATED NEWSPAPER FOR THE HOME With which is incorporated "BLACK & WHITE"

Volume LIX. No. 779. {REGISTERED AT THE GENERAL POST OFFICE AS A NEWSPAPER} London, December 26 1914. Price Sixpence.

DRAWN BY F. MATANIA FROM A SKETCH BY G. H. DAVIS AT HARTLEPOOL

THE BOMBARDMENT OF THE EAST COAST—THE SCENE OUTSIDE A HARTLEPOOL BAPTIST CHAPEL

offered excellent photographic opportunities. When based in Britain, the Australian, New Zealand, and Canadian forces were all frequently photographed and occasionally, on their own initiative, had a professional attached for a longer period to accumulate the record of their service overseas. The arrival of the first American troops was brought forward to June 1917 for its much-needed morale effect and they were assured of publicity. Admiration for their strength and smartness in training, at drill, and on ceremonial occasions seemed to be a universal reaction.

From covering the direct participants in war the press turned to its casualties; the refugees, the prisoners, and the wounded. At first there was enormous sympathy for the plight of the Belgians who arrived in their thousands as their country fell to the Germans in the autumn of 1914. The recurrent theme of 'little Belgium' falling victim to the foul 'Hun' had obvious potential for photographic presentation of the difficulties of tired and confused refugees and the necessity to organize collections to house, clothe, and feed them (*plate d*). Later, relations were to be strained by the inevitable differences of outlook but for the moment these were forgotten in the generation of anti-German feeling.

Prisoners were a subject of some ambivalence; they were part of a nation which stood accused of some brutal outrages but as members of its fighting forces were loyal and patriotic soldiers. They were also a measure of success to their captors. In the trenches there was often a good deal of respect between the opposing sides and it certainly became the host nation to treat its prisoners in the civilized manner which it purported to be fighting to defend. However, popular feeling, incited by atrocity stories and the general impression of the 'brutal Hun' could be suspicious of their presence. At the officers' camp at Donnington Hall in Derbyshire the standard of comfort drew criticism. Photographs were published showing the pleasant rooms and attractive grounds in what had been a grand house (*plate f*). The War Office had to confirm that restrictions were applied just as much there as anywhere. But the emphasis on the captors' superior humanity continued; the *Daily Mirror*'s photographs of the first prisoners arriving at Southampton after the battle of the Somme in 1916 made great play of generosity with the twin essentials of the aftermath of battle, cigarettes and water.

Nursing the injured was one of the traditional roles of women in wartime, but the number of the casualties and the appalling nature of their wounds caused by artillery and poison gas meant a huge increase in the profession. Amongst the aristocracy not only was nursing deemed a ladylike way of helping the war effort but their large houses could provide extensive if at times inconvenient accommodation. Picturesque photographs of former great houses showing wards with glittering chandeliers and impressive paintings housing convalescent patients were a staple of illustrated articles and usually included a glowing tribute to the benefactor. But despite their smiles the bitter hurt of the wounded was often revealed in the appalling accumulation of their loss of limbs. It is difficult to gauge the impact of these photographs with their implicit tragedy contradicting their determined cheerfulness as the casualties of war became a commonplace of everyday life (*plate o*). Certainly, this type of material was not published in the early stages when for the most part the tone was anodyne. The relationship between the soldiers and the civilians was assumed to be more distant, with the latter providing moral support and relaxation rather than being direct participants; the *Daily Mirror*'s photograph of a soldier and his girlfriends sledging at Epsom over the Christmas holidays of 1914 epitomized this assumption which the naval bombardment of towns on the east coast in 1914 and the aerial raids which began in January 1915 were fundamentally to alter (*plate e*).

Britain was startled and horrified that the German Navy should level its guns against Scarborough and Hartlepool on 16 December 1914. By later standards casualties were light, just over 100, but because they were the first deliberately caused civilian deaths they were reported in tones of outrage. Photographs of the damage to property were widely published with extensive indictments of German iniquity and where they failed for obvious reasons to show the actual incidents the deficiency was made good with drawings which could by judicious combination depict the misdeeds against women and children, homes and churches (*plate g*). In January 1915 Germany launched a series of raids by Zeppelin airships on London which, although their actual effect was slight in terms of loss of life or serious damage to property, caused widespread panic and alarm. In response the government decreed that only official statements were to be published and took the unprecedented step of directly linking them with official photographs. The firm of Walsham's Ltd which usually serviced the needs of the Office of Works at the Home Office agreed to undertake a special series showing the harm done. These tended to be used with headlines such as 'Dastard Work of the Kaiser's Air Pirates' and 'In the Track of the Zeppelin Murderers'.[1] The obvious failure of the aerial defences in London and other cities which came under attack in 1916 and 1917 caused a storm of criticism so it was inevitable that their first success, the shooting down of the airship, Shutte-Lanz 11 (SL 11) by Lieutenant William Leefe Robinson flying a BE 2c of 39 Home Defence Squadron over Cuffley in Hertfordshire on 2–3 September 1916, should attract tremendous interest. Leefe Robinson was awarded the Victoria Cross, the only one to be won for action in Britain, and at twenty-one became a hero. His photograph and those of the huge skeletal remains of the airship were prominently featured in the press and the whole episode was treated with more than a touch of the apocalyptic; an eye-witness account in the *Daily Mail*[2] read:

> The silver thing in the sky moved, turned, rose. It seemed to tremble. It had gone. The sky seemed to come down between it and us. Then the firing of the guns stopped. We seemed to be talking very loudly. . . . Then suddenly with incalculable swiftness, the whole of

(*h*) Firemen hosing down Cox's Court in the City of London after an air raid in 1917. Walsham's Ltd for the Home Office, HO 77.

(*i*) A woman using the huge machinery involved in the making of cartridge cases; a Ministry of Munitions photograph. *The Sphere*, 4 May 1918.

THE SPHERE

AN ILLUSTRATED NEWSPAPER FOR THE HOME — *With which is incorporated "BLACK & WHITE"*

Volume LXXIII. No. 954. { REGISTERED AT THE GENERAL POST OFFICE AS A NEWSPAPER } London, May 4, 1918. Price One Shilling and Sixpence.

By courtesy of the Ministry of Munitions

IN A MUNITION FACTORY—A WOMAN MAKING 4·5 CARTRIDGE CASES

the sky was lit up with a great flame. The stars were gone. The sky had become a sheet of crimson. It was like the miracles which are older than the world. I could not look at it. Then somewhere I heard people shouting. The sound of it seemed to rise out of the earth. But it seemed to come from the mouth of a great multitude.

However, success seemed slow in coming against the attacks being carried out by large aircraft, the Gothas, against London in 1917 and the morale of the war-weary population dipped badly. Walsham's still assiduously recorded the damage sustained but its release seems to have been less favoured than photographs of the growing network of defences, the anti-aircraft guns and Home Defence squadrons of the Royal Flying Corps. The threat petered out after February 1918 and attention was turned to other matters.

For the civilian 1916 was the year when the war, which had been an affair for volunteers and a matter of slight domestic inconvenience, began to touch the whole nation. Conscription was introduced on a limited basis in January 1916 and made universal in May, the new Ministry of Munitions introduced official control to the armaments industry, and shortages of domestic goods caused by the demands of the war economy and the toll of merchant shipping in the submarine war became marked. A system of voluntary rationing was introduced in early 1917 but was rapidly abandoned in favour of imposed ration cards and coupons. The illustrated press began to explore the implications of a nation turning over the bulk of its resources to war, and in particular to cover the extension of the role of women in industry and the forces. As men were called up for active service, women took over many of their roles in the process known as 'substitution'. *The Sphere* was typical in its coverage of this theme which was especially relevant to the munitions industry. Its cover illustration for 3 July 1915 automatically showed men at work around the furnace in which noses of shells were finished off, but on 4 May 1918 an official Ministry of Munitions photograph was used showing a woman solely responsible for a huge piece of machinery which made cartridge cases (*plate i*). The caption emphasized that 'This is only one of the many operations connected with the making of munitions which are being successfully carried out by women.' During 1917 women were shown with increasing frequency undertaking jobs previously considered entirely masculine: in munition factories, paper mills, metal works, brickyards, and on the railways and trams. Their role in agriculture in organizations such as the Land Army was also included as domestic food production became more important to a restricted island economy. The photographs were often accompanied by information on how to join the various organizations involved.

It was quite novel for women to wear any sort of uniform and so as they entered the new auxiliary forces in increasing numbers they attracted a good deal of attention. Women donned uniform in transport, nursing, agricultural, and eventually military organizations. The

Women's Army Auxiliary Corps was founded in July 1917, the Women's Royal Naval Service in November of the same year, and the Women's Royal Auxiliary Air Force on 1 April 1918. They provided a rich field for photography. *The Sphere* produced a special issue on 4 May 1918 devoted almost entirely to the phenomenon of women at war and introduced it:

> A modern Rip Van Winkle falling asleep in those far-off days of peace and waking in the present day, might well rub his eyes in amazement at the war-time change which has come over our English Eve. Four years – or nearly – of war have made her free of the most jealously-guarded masculine preserves; she has entered practically all the professions, she has discarded her petticoats, she has a vote.[3]

The photographs used for this and similar articles were taken either by press photographers working on a permit basis, by professionals commissioned for the government organization concerned such as the Ministry of Munitions, or in the case of the distinguished ladies involved were often portraits drawn from existing stock.

However, as the prosecution of the war was increasingly dependent on the contribution of the civilian it seemed an obvious ploy to include the home front in official propaganda. Although the supply of photographs from the battlefields remained its main concern, in 1917 the newly upgraded Department of Information began to consider including the civilian in official photography. In the event, although a certain amount of material was sent abroad and published at home, the impulse to provide propaganda was diverted by the involvement of an additional organization, the newly founded Imperial War Museum, towards the permanent record.

The first full-time official photographer of the home front was Horace Nicholls, an established professional who had made his reputation during the Boer War. Appointed in July 1917 he was granted the resounding title 'Official Photographer of Great Britain' but the letter[4] confirming this showed that the Department was still far from considering mass circulation; his work would be used in a series of books and not released to the British press. In fact this restriction was rapidly overcome in view of the demand for material. One of his earliest assignments was to tour the great munition and ordnance factories where he took a memorable series of photographs which conveyed the scale of operations, the number of workers, and the growing skill of the women recruits at the technical detail of their jobs. Unlike the majority of photographers of the day he liked to work round his chosen theme and build up a 'story' on subjects such as enlistment, a soldier's leave, and the events of the women workers' day.

By early 1918, the upgraded Ministry of Information was anxious to supplement Nicholls' efforts and in April appointed its other full-time professional, G. P. Lewis. He was blessed with a sanguine temperament and strong determination, excellent qualities for a

(*j*) Munitions: men and women painting the massive array of shells in production at the largest shell-filling factory in Britain at Chilwell *c.* 1918. British official, Horace Nicholls, Q 30018.

(*k*) Agriculture: a Land Army girl milks a cow. The original caption read 'a gleam of sunshine in the cowshed'. British official, Horace Nicholls, Q 30681.

(*l*) Transport: a Glasgow tram driver and conductor wearing their smart tartan uniform. British official, G. P. Lewis, Q 28389.

(*m*) Women in uniform: an inspector and sergeant in the Women's Police Service. British official, Horace Nicholls, Q 30339.

(*n*) The professions: a woman dentist carrying out treatment. British official, Horace Nicholls, Q 30851.

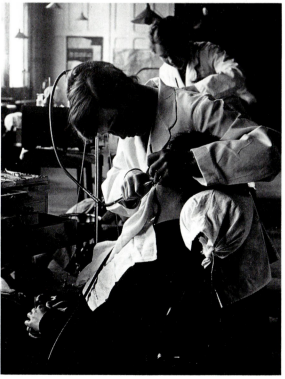

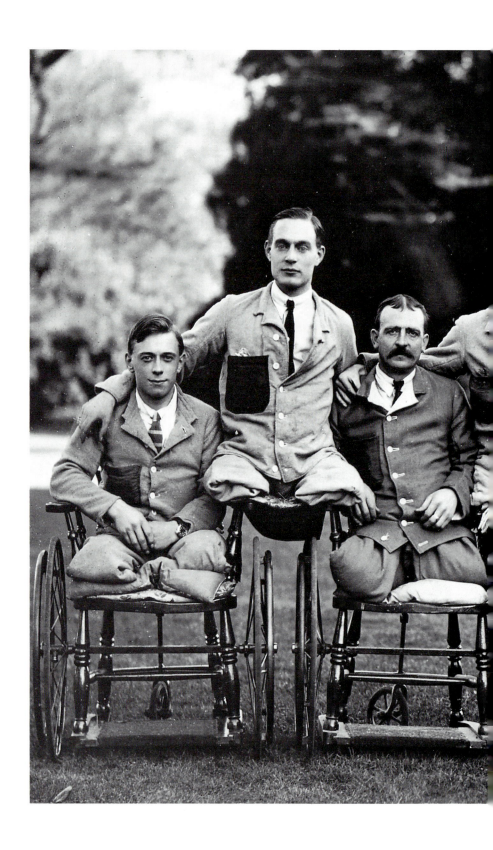

(*o*) A pitiable sight which became increasingly common: limbless veterans at Roehampton Military Hospital. Professional photograph, British Red Cross Society, Q 108161.

photographer who was to travel much of the length and breadth of Britain. Like Nicholls, one of his early commissions involved munitions, in his case at the Royal Arsenal at Woolwich, and he also devoted a good deal of time to his portfolio on the work of the Women's Royal Naval Service which was carried out with a view to the permanent national record as well as immediate publication.

In early 1918 the momentum gathered behind the proposal which had been agreed in Cabinet in March 1917 to found an Imperial War Museum, and its various committees were avidly collecting whatever they could. It had been established from the beginning that it would be not only tri-service but include the role of civilians, especially the women's contribution, and its Women's Work Committee set out to gather material. Its formidable lady members attacked their task with a good deal of energy and ability. Looking for suitable records they found plenty of impressive statistics but insufficient visual illustrations. They decided to encourage interest and acquisition by arranging an exhibition in the autumn of 1918. After some harassed negotiation they secured the services of both Nicholls and Lewis in co-operation with the Ministry of Information. The former embarked on a series of portraits of women in uniform, ranging through the military, nursing, police, transport, and agricultural services to the overalls worn by female war office clerks. He had the ability to make women relax in front of his camera and while many of his sitters were past the first bloom of youth they always appeared full of character. He also portrayed women in the professions and in the hard manual jobs such as chimney sweeping and coke heaving where increasing numbers were substituting for men. Besides these, he also photographed women involved in agriculture and here his romantic idealism could be clearly seen. His own suggestions to describe them confirm his approach; 'A gleam of sunshine in the cowshed' described a girl busy milking a cow (*plate k*), 'Setting in the fall' a forestry worker with the sun in her hair, and 'Comme il faut' a land girl chatting to a good-looking American soldier on a summer evening. In his turn Lewis travelled extensively working on similar themes, specializing in heavy manufacture, and portraying workers in the glass, coal, gas, paper, leather, and food industries. In Glasgow where he complained that 'it rained cats and dogs'[5] all the time he was very taken with the smart tartan uniform of the women drivers and conductors on the trams (*plate l*). On the whole he had a less sentimental approach than Nicholls, although it was a consistent assumption in both men's work that their subjects were, without exception, willing, eager, and able to contribute to the national effort.

After an arduous summer for both men, the ladies of the War Museum Committee, and the much pressed officials of the Ministry of Information, many of the photographs were included in a very successful exhibition at the Whitechapel galleries and later became part of the national archive. The official photographers of the home front had in effect been diverted for most of the period of their appointments to working along very different lines to those elsewhere. They were not primarily concerned with the production of news photographs, nor even of material for possible release to the press at some later date but first and foremost with compiling a record. The impetus of the Women's Work Committee seems to have driven the Ministry of Information to accomplish rather more than it would have done otherwise, given its preoccupation with the supply of photographs from the theatres of war and its late appreciation of the civilian as a participant in the war effort.

The broadening role of the civilian in war was reflected in photography generally. Instead of being a bystander in the traditional role of moral supporter or nurse, he and particularly she, became an active participant in the effort essential to continue. The First World War was the occasion when civilians at home began to feel part of another theatre of war, equally engrossed in its prosecution and as liable to attack. For women especially, the changes were dramatic although the expansion of their role did not survive the economic disasters of the twenties and thirties. However, the potential of the photograph as an aid to persuasion or encouragement by example was hardly explored at all in official terms, not only because of the concentration of limited resources elsewhere but also by the diversion of the official photographers to the national record. The fact that the Ministry condoned and even encouraged this diversion showed how far removed it still remained from a sustained campaign of deliberate influence based on photographs. In fact without particular prompting the press gathered ample material to demonstrate and encourage the extension of the civilians' role and, by doing so, underlined the continuing consensus of the war effort.

7

CONCLUSION

The First World War was the first major conflict to have a contemporary photographic iconography, a large part of which was preserved as national records. It was established through the use of official, professional, and private material in the press and its subsequent incorporation into the archives of the countries concerned. The balance between these categories of photographs reflected the precedence of and priorities within the different theatres of war and, as it went on, the development of the official photograph as the main source of topical illustrative material. The greater direction of the imperial war effort was mirrored in the increasing control of visual information but its application varied considerably. The Gallipoli operation saw the first experiments with the concept of official photography while on the Western Front, the most important and most static theatre, conditions favoured its fullest development. On the fringes in Egypt, Palestine, and Mesopotamia there was room for the unorthodox but in the war at sea, the Royal Navy remained chary of publicity and had the capacity to evade it easily. Not until the second half of the war was photography of the civilian contribution seriously considered by the official propaganda organization and then it was diverted by circumstance more towards the national record. The independent professional press photographer was excluded, except for occasional exceptional circumstances, from the most important battle area, the Western Front, deterred by expense from serious consideration of the outer theatres of war, barred from the ships of the Royal Navy, and curtailed by the permit system from undertaking subjects relevant to the military effort on the home front. The amateur's circumstances varied; he might find his work sought after for publication in the early months on the Western Front, or if he was present during a naval action, or serving in Mesopotamia, but otherwise he might be forbidden to use his camera altogether or expected to confine himself to purely personal usage of it. Publication of amateur material became very infrequent as the war went on and the supply of official photographs grew.

The upshot was that the official photographers had the best opportunities to provide a comprehensive view of the war in terms of photography of its action, its support services, and its cost but their accomplishment was severely limited by their numbers. There were

(*a*) A publicity photograph of 'Tommy Atkins' taken and published to show the 'Spirit of Play Still Dancing the Wake of War' in *The War Illustrated*, 25 May 1918, during the German offensive. British official, John Warwick Brooke, Q 6536.

140

only sixteen permanent appointments in all the various theatres, although as time went on assistants for darkroom work and driving duties were available and there were several shortlived additions to the main photographic strength. Some 40,000 photographs were taken under official auspices, of which some 30,000 were British, 5,000 Australian, and 4,000 Canadian. The bulk of these came from the Western Front: 20,000 British, 4,000 Australian, and all the Canadian material. Other theatres lagged far behind; official photographs of the war at sea numbered some 2,000, with about the same from Mesopotamia but only 600 from Egypt. Approximately 3,000 photographs were taken on the home front. As the longest serving official photographer, Ernest Brooks took about 4,400, closely followed by John Warwick Brooke with 4,100, with William Rider-Rider not far behind. Unfortunately, the individual attributions to the Australians did not survive. For four years of war it was a relatively small total.[1] It demonstrated clearly how much was ruled out by the simple restriction of numbers. Even in the main theatre of war on the Western Front photography was a matter of practicalities about transport and information rather than contrivance over the choice of subject. Directives from London tended to be simply hopeful urgings for greater quantity and more variety. Censorship was carried out after the photographs were taken and although obsessive about the details of military or naval security, which might reveal the identification of a unit or place, remained essentially a passive role.

Compared to other systems of official photography, the British effort was tiny; on the Western Front alone, Germany, anxious to present her campaigns in the best possible light and the technical leader in photography generally, maintained an average of about fifty operators; and France, concerned to sustain the national effort against the invader, had approximately thirty-five. Both countries had far greater opportunity to direct their photographers towards particular themes which suited declared propagandist intentions, although German material was on occasion so obviously manipulated that it lost credibility. The British press, in the absence of an adequate supply from its own forces, made frequent recourse to photographs from foreign, especially French, sources.

Fundamental to British official photography was its principle of 'the propaganda of the facts' and its attempt to maintain the equation of official and authoritative. Although some scene setting was acceptable, outright faking of action or tampering with the results was definitely not. As a result its status was rarely questioned. As far as can be established the great bulk of official photographs that were taken were published with only occasional alteration of technical detail as part of the contemporary account of the war. This success showed not only the predictable demand but the common, if not necessarily acknowledged, assumptions of those involved at all levels. But as the small size of the operation ruled out any elaborate directives the photographers in the field fell back on their professional training and as a large proportion

(*b*) The commemoration of sacrifice: the coffin of the 'Unknown Warrior' lying in state in Westminster Abbey before its burial during the Armistice Day service of 11 November 1920. Horace Nicholls, Q 31514.

of them were drawn from the same newspaper it can be suggested that it, rather than the propaganda or military organizations, was the consistent influence on the choice of subject and style of photography, certainly on the Western Front. Before the war the *Daily Mirror* had led the field in pictorial journalism in newspapers. Of the dozen men on the Western Front, 'Bart' Bartholomew, Ernest Brooks, Ivor Castle, David McClellan, and William Rider-Rider were all former employees. The paper was firmly based on its popular appeal which in wartime became a mustering of patriotic sentiment, reassurance, and morale-bracing stories. Given the problems of access to and difficulties of taking successful pictures in the front line, and the unlikelihood of publication of photographs of the dead which offended contemporary standards of decency, the inclination of the photographers was to concentrate on those items of human interest which the paper had found to have such a wide attraction: the endearing ordinariness of 'Tommy Atkins', his loyalty to King and Country, his cheerfulness in the face of discomfort, and his fondness for games, children, and pets. Variety was provided by photographs of the picturesque and unusual. Their heroes remained anonymous and the ideal of the nation, or more immediately the military unit, took precedence over the individual and there was little room for the cult of personality. This reached its apotheosis after the war when, in order to commemorate the sacrifice and the thousands with no known grave, it was decided to bury an 'unknown warrior' with full honours in Westminster Abbey after the Armistice Day service of 11 November 1920 (*plate b*).

In presenting the photographs of the war, the illustrated press accompanied them with extensive captions detailing their implications. The pictorial was not regarded as an equal or potentially superior partner of the written word and the shorthand in visual communication currently taken for granted remained untried. The pivot of the presentation remained literary. This was also determined by the way the photographers worked and their need to make their supply of negative plates go as far as possible. They tended to think in terms of single images as being sufficient and there was hardly any attempt to link the photographs directly with each other or with an accompanying narrative until they arrived on the editor's desk, hence the profusion of words to interpret and link often disparate material. The photographers also assumed that they should concentrate on being as close to the battle as possible. On the Western Front the military installation of headquarters, training grounds, repair shops, camps, stores, roads, and railways, was bigger than London but it was barely hinted at in the photographs. It was in the text that the obvious slanting and emotive presentation occurred. Many were used to demonstrate the popular stereotypes of the period such as 'Tommy Atkins', and their ambivalence must be realized. But they showed with sometimes surprising clarity the mud and misery of the front line. It was apparent, despite the pleasantries of some of their presentations, that life on the Western Front was a horrifying experience with death at the soldier's elbow. But, although the tone of the press altered drastically from its early optimism to sober perseverance, the change reflected rather than led public opinion. The basic consensus of the nation that the war had to be fought and won survived until the end. Reaction came later. In retrospect it seems unlikely that the case for halting the conflict because of visual evidence of its waste of life would have found a hearing any earlier, even had the photographers considered it their role to provide this point of view which they emphatically did not. They did not consider themselves independent observers of the struggle but privileged participants whose skill was being put to patriotic use.

For the rest of the century the development of war photography can be seen in terms of the tension between the growing status and independence of the war photographer and the attempt of the military, at least in the free press of democracies, to come to terms with it. The development of the small, compact 35mm camera, led by the revolutionary design of the Leica in 1925, gave the photographer discretion as well as mobility and capacity. He could observe and record with unprecedented candour, experiment, and afford failure. The concept of deliberate preparation of words and photographs by a journalist and photographer working together was explored and a new style of reporting, dubbed photo-journalism, grew. It originated in Germany but the American magazine, *Life*, founded in 1936, was one of its most successful exponents. The photographer now enjoyed a creative rather than a craftsman's role.

But for the military, reporting remained an activity requiring control; during the Second World War the apparatus of official information was revived and hugely expanded to meet the proliferation of media. Unlike the First World War the official effort did not attempt to be exclusive. The services and the home front had official photographers generating publicity material but professionals of their own and other countries were also allowed access. The term 'official', which had become somewhat discredited after the First World War as the gap between the official communiqués and the history of the struggle became apparent, was further tarnished by the inept handling of material in the early days of the re-formed Ministry of Information. However, once again official photographers had the best opportunities and their work was once more a staple of press supply for news of battle. Apart from the sheer quantity, some two million photographs in the Second compared to the 40,000 of the First, the main differences between the official images of the two world wars lay in the more candid observation and the personalization of the visual account of the Second. They also pushed back the ever-widening parameters of what it was acceptable to publish on the atrocity of war. Few images have had quite the impact of the photographs taken of the liberation of the concentration camps and the appalling revelation of their contents.

The status of the war photographer reached a peak in the late sixties during the Vietnam War. Here in this American imbroglio in south-

(*c*) Dead Germans in a trench during the 1917 battles on the Western Front, an unpublishable photograph by contemporary standards. British official, Ernest Brooks, Q 3117.

(*d*) Evidence of atrocity: bodies left to rot in Belsen concentration camp, April 1945. British official, BU 3755.

(*e*) Vietnamese civilians injured by American hand grenades in Hué, 1968. Don McCullin, courtesy of the Victoria and Albert Museum.

east Asia a medley of professionals, hangers-on, and ex-hippies enjoyed a unique degree of privileged access. Their photographs, such as those taken by Don McCullin, revealed the grim bitterness of a losing fight against an elusive enemy and marked the final shift of the photographer from patriot to witness against war. But the history of press involvement in Vietnam was not calculated to inspire confidence between the military and the media, and in the most recent British conflict, the Falklands War, much older attitudes resurfaced; the Royal Navy displayed its traditional reluctance to allow reporting. The sheer physical distance of the Falkland Islands from Britain made it especially awkward to accommodate supernumeraries, but in many ways the particular problems of the few press photographers accredited to the Task Force echoed those of the relationships of the First World War but with the added complication that in 1982 the photographers expected to preserve their independence.

During the First World War there was growing recognition for the status of the topical photograph as a news medium, a contribution to propaganda, a popular souvenir, a work of art in exhibition, and as

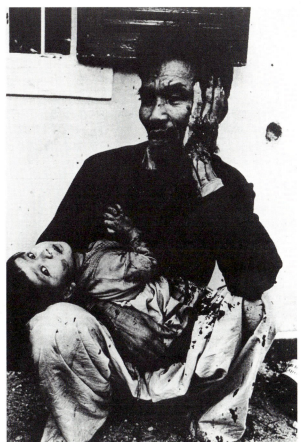

an item for inclusion in a national archive, but there was little for its taker, the photographer. War correspondents had an established professional tradition and their work was easily reproduced in the press, the paintings and drawings of the war artists were at once appreciated for their significance in offering a distillation of human experience, while the new industry of film-makers could produce a novel and self-contained product with immense mass appeal. The photographer was accustomed to his work being incorporated as part of a general layout for publication and his role remained that of a craftsman providing a service rather than an individual achievement. The names of the official war correspondents and artists became well known but the official photographers remained more or less anonymous.

Slowly the press began to relinquish its conservative preference for the written and artistic and to make more use of the photograph particularly in war serial publications. But war was and is an especially difficult subject to photograph in terms of items of news, as what is in front of the camera is inevitably only part of the whole and can be extremely monotonous. Complaints of repetition and shortage were inevitable given the restriction of sources. The official propaganda organization in its various guises found photographs increasingly important in its work and, although it could not gauge clearly the effect of circulation, it could not do without them. They became an essential part of the effort to contradict the enemy and influence nations in Britain's favour. They also marked the transition from an appeal to the few to the masses.

The status of photographs was further enhanced by their fairly frequent exhibition in various art galleries where they proved immensely popular. Beaverbrook had been one of the first to organize such displays and on more than one occasion the British official photographers were moved to complain about the prominence given to Canadian material, especially the work of the rather disliked Ivor Castle. On show in such a venue, the official photograph gained something of the respect usually accorded a work of art, much above that given to its publication in the illustrated press, but the name of the photographer rarely accompanied it.

It was in October 1918 that the Ministry of Information decided to take advantage of popular demand and opened a shop for the sale of official photographs to the public on its premises in Coventry Street. They had enjoyed considerable success in the form of postcards produced under licence by the *Daily Mail* and had also been incorporated, together with other material, into the sets of stereoscopic prints covering the story of the war produced in quantity by firms such as Underwood & Underwood and Realistic Travels. The Ministry hoped for similar success and although it was transformed on 1 January 1919 into the Department of Photographs of the Imperial War Museum, the practice of selling copies had proved its popularity and still continues.

The establishment of a national record had been a consideration,

although of differing priority, underlying much of British and Imperial official photography. This was most clearly demonstrated on the Western Front; the efforts of Charles Bean ensured that the Australian record was as comprehensive and carefully documented as possible, the Canadian account owed most to one skilled and conscientious photographer, William Rider-Rider, trying to encompass both the topical and the historical, while the British, their few men always at a stretch, inevitably put pressing demands for the former first. Their descriptions, hurriedly written and poorly detailed, were adequate for publication but not for the proper historical record. In the outer theatres the photographers worked in isolation with little concern for the ultimate fate of their work once it had been safely dispatched to London, while in the Royal Navy the permanent record of its role was only considered after the event. In contrast, nearly all the official photography of the home front was done with a view to the long term.

(*f*) One of the few photographs of the moment of attack: an officer leads the way out of a sap during the spring battles of 1918. British official, John Warwick Brooke, Q 5100.

Canada had established a national archive when it became a dominion in the 1860s but the Imperial and Australian War Museums were both founded in early 1917 as part of the impetus to commemorate the war. Their contribution to the First World War had profoundly altered the relationship between the larger dominions and the mother country. Instead of being dependants of doubtful capacity, they became participants with a national integrity of their own. It was an important stage in their development as nations. The regular publication of photographs emphasizing their achievements and national characteristics could not but reinforce the perception of their separate identity, confirmed by their inclusion in their countries' national records.

But the national archives threw their net wider than just the official photographs; they recognized the importance to the visual record of the personal experience of war and aimed to gather as many private collections as possible. It was the first time that photographs of the ordinary individual had been thought worthy of preservation in this way. The amateurs' contribution was enormously important in the

narrative of otherwise unrecorded areas, events, and campaigns, their accumulation of the variety of individual experience of war, and their genuinely casual and candid photography.

The inclusion of photographs from other sources in national archives pointed to the shortcomings of the Imperial record of the First World War; not nearly as many photographs were taken as technically could have been. However, the power of the still image lies not only in its description of the immediate but also in its capacity to suggest and symbolize. With the benefit of hindsight and understanding of context, many of the photographs are potent evocations of the experience and the cost of war. To modern eyes, a line of men advancing in single file might imply not just that particular battle but the continuous colossal demand for manpower in the infantry throughout the war, besides their bravery in facing the fusillades of ammunition. Photographs of devastated landscapes once published as evidence of victory seem to epitomize the futility of those four years of struggle. Overall the photographs of the First World War show the beginning in earnest of the transition of photography from a technical or artistic ploy for the

(g) Symbols of the First World War: wounded men and German prisoners making their way through the wasted ground of the battlefield at Passchendaele 1917. Canadian official, William Rider-Rider, CO 2190.

(*h*) Symbols of the First World War: the line of the infantry going forward in the last stages of the 1918 offensive. British official, David McClellan, Q 9236.

individual in the nineteenth century to a medium of far-reaching import for the masses in the twentieth. During the war the tensions between the capacity of the camera and control of its output restricted numbers rather than content and in the end the technical skill of the professional and the intimate work of the amateur combined as never before to create its lasting and powerful photographic record.

NOTES

1   Photographic opportunities

1 The first head of section was Ernest Gowers but he was replaced after only a few weeks by Ivor Nicholson.
2 Entry for 13 June 1917 quoted in Janet Adam-Smith, *John Buchan*, Rupert Hart Davis, London, 1965, p. 170.

2   Uncertain beginnings

1 IWM/Photos, Christopher Pilkington corres.; the name of the officer is not given.
2 IWM/Docs, Diary of Christopher Pilkington.
3 IWM/Photos, J. Selby Grigg corres.
4 IWM/Docs, Mairi Chisholm papers.

3   Official control

1 Quoted in 'Q744' by R. B. Grundy, *Stand To, The Journal of the Western Front Association*, Summer 1986, no. 17, p. 10.
2 Lieutenant William Rider-Rider, 'With a camera at the Front', *Canada in Khaki*, no. 3, London, 1919, pp. 107–8.
3 William Rider-Rider, interview, cited in Peter Robinson, 'Canadian photojournalism during the First World War', *History of Photography*, vol. 2, no. 1, 1978.
4 G. H. Wilkins was known in later life as Sir Hubert Wilkins, knighted for his pioneering of Polar flying.
5 Hurley's diary quoted in Lennard Bickel, *In Search of Frank Hurley*, Sydney, Macmillan of Australia, 1980, p. 61.
6 After the war H. G. Bartholomew returned to the *Daily Mirror* where he became editor and later chairman of the *Mirror* group.

4   Unorthodox achievement

1 IWM/MOI papers; George Westmoreland personal file.
2 Colour photographs now held by the Australian War Memorial. For reproductions see Lennard Bickel, *In Search of Frank Hurley*, Sydney, Macmillan of Australia, 1980.
3 IWM/Docs, L. S. Bell Syer diary.

5   Traditional silence

1 *Indiscretions of the Naval Censor*, Rear Admiral Sir Douglas Brownrigg, Cassell & Co., London, 1920, p. 40.

2 ibid., p. 152.
3 ibid., p. 14.
4 IWM/Photos; introduction to *Women in Shipbuilding* albums.
5 IWM/HU 51900 and HU 51899.
6 G. P. Lewis, christian name George, always known professionally as G. P. Lewis.
7 Quoted *The Illustrated London News*, 4 May 1918.
8 Admiralty order no. 1542.

6   *A new participant*

1 *The War Illustrated*, 30 October 1915.
2 Also quoted in *The Sphere*, 9 September 1916.
3 Women over 30 had been given the vote on 6 February 1918.
4 IWM/MOI papers, Horace Nicholls personal file.
5 IWM/MOI papers, G. P. Lewis personal file.

7   *Conclusion*

1 All these figures should be regarded as very approximate because of the difficulty in many cases of determining exact provenance.

OUTLINE CHRONOLOGY

1914

28 June: Assassination of the Archduke Francis Ferdinand, heir to the Austro-Hungarian empire at Sarajevo, Serbia.

28 July: Austria–Hungary declares war on Serbia and on the following day Russia orders a partial mobilization as a gesture in support of the Serbs.

4 August: Great Britain declares war on Germany. Britain, France, and Russia are now the main allied 'Entente Powers' preparing to fight Germany and Austria–Hungary, the main 'Central Powers'.

7 August: First units of the British Expeditionary Force arrive in France.

23–4 August: BEF retreats from Mons.

28 August: Naval action of Heligoland Bight.

September: British garrison force in Egypt strengthened.

19 October–22 November: First battle of Ypres, the lines of the opposing armies on the Western Front stabilize.

1 November: Turkey enters the war as Germany's ally. From 6 November the Indian Expeditionary Force D occupies Basra at the head of the Persian Gulf.

1 November: Naval battle of Coronel.

8 December: Naval battle of the Falkland Islands.

16 December: German naval bombardment of Scarborough and Hartlepool.

1915

19 January: First Zeppelin raid on Britain.

19 February–18 March: Naval bombardment of the Dardanelles.

10–13 March: Battle of Neuve Chapelle.

22 April–5 May: Second battle of Ypres.

25 April: First landings of the Mediterranean Expeditionary Force at Gallipoli.

9 May: Start of combined allied offensive, includes Aubers Ridge, Artois, and Festubert, on the Western Front.

6–15 August: Further landings at Suvla on the Gallipoli peninsula fail.

25 September–8 October: Allied autumn offensive; battle of Loos.

19 December: General Sir Douglas Haig appointed Commander-in-Chief of the British Armies in France in succession to Field Marshal Sir John French.

1916

8 January: Evacuation from Gallipoli completed.

24 January: Conscription introduced in Britain on a limited basis by the Military Services Bill and made universal on 16 May.

21 February–31 August: Siege of Verdun.

31 May–1 June: Naval battle of Jutland.

5 June: Sherif Hussein declares Arab revolt against Turkish rule.

1 July–18 November: Battle of the Somme.

29 November: Admiral Sir David Beatty succeeds Admiral Sir John Jellicoe as Commander-in-Chief of the Royal Navy.

7 December: David Lloyd George replaces H. H. Asquith as Prime Minister of the national coalition government.

1917

January: T. E. Lawrence, attached to Sherif Hussein's forces as an adviser, begins guerrilla operations in the Hejaz.

1 February: Germany declares unrestricted submarine warfare.

11 March: Fall of Baghdad to British forces.

12 March: Russian revolution begins.

26 March: First battle of Gaza, British advance into Palestine is halted.

6 April: USA declares war on Germany.

9 April–4 May: Battle of Arras.

21 May–7 June: Battle of Messines.

25 June: First American contingent arrives in France.

31 July–10 November: Third battle of Ypres (Passchendaele).

24 October: Bolsheviks seize power in Russia.

27 October–7 November: Gaza taken, British advance into Palestine continues.

20 November: Battle of Cambrai.

3 December: Capture of Jerusalem.

17 December: Armistice between Russia and the Central Powers.

1918

3 March: Russia withdraws from the war in European and Turkish theatres in the Treaty of Brest-Litovsk.

21 March: Opening of German offensive against the British on the Western Front.

12 April: Field Marshal Sir Douglas Haig issues 'backs to the wall' Order of the Day to the army in France.

22/23 April: Naval raid on the submarine bases at Zeebrugge, and on 9/10 May on those at Ostend.

8 August: Beginning of successful Allied stand and counter-attack at the battle of Amiens.

19 September: Battle of Megiddo begins in Palestine.

26 September: Allied attack on the Western Front pushes the German army back behind its own defence system, the Hindenburg Line.

30 October: Armistice with Turkey.

11 November: Armistice with Germany.

THE PHOTOGRAPHERS

Summary of official and private photographers mentioned

Official photographers

Here are listed the most important of the official photographers and their main spheres of activity. The list is not exhaustive as it does not include several minor appointments nor those who worked regularly on a permit per assignment basis on the home front.

Aitken, Thomas (Tom) Keith	British official, Western Front
Baldwin, Herbert	Australian official, Western Front
Brooke, John Warwick	British official, Western Front
Brooks, Ernest	British official, Gallipoli, Western Front, Italy, and occasional work for the Admiralty
Castle, William Ivor	Canadian official, Western Front and occasional Admiralty work
Consolé, Armando	British official, Western Front
Hurley, Frank	Australian nationality, Australian official, Western Front and Palestine
Knobel, Harry Edward	Canadian nationality, Canadian official, Western Front
Lewis, G. P. (George)	British official, Western Front
McClellan, David	British official, Home Front
Nicholls, Horace W.	British official, Home Front
Rider-Rider, William	Canadian official, Western Front
Scales, Thomas	New Zealand official, Western Front
Varges, Ariel	American nationality, British official, Mesopotamia
Westmoreland, George	British official, Egypt and Palestine
Wilkins, George Hubert	Australian nationality, Australian official, Western Front (later Sir Hubert Wilkins)

Private photographers

Acland, Captain Wilfred Dyke	pioneer of naval aviation
Bean, Captain C. E. W.	Australian official correspondent and historian, used personal camera at Gallipoli
Byrne, Colonel Stanley	commanded 1/11 London Regiment, Egypt and Palestine
Cane, Major A. S.	Royal Army Medical Corps, siege of Kut
Chisholm, Mairi	with the Baroness de T'Serclaes (Mrs Elsie Knocker), the 'Women of Pervyse', who ran their first-aid post in the Belgian front line

159

Duckworth, Lieutenant A.	HMS *Invincible*
Jacobs, Captain H.	1st Battalion, Anzac, Gallipoli
Lawrence, T. E.	'Lawrence of Arabia', attached as military adviser to Emir Feisal's forces in Arabia
Money, Lieutenant R. C.	1st Battalion Cameronians, Western Front
Pilkington, Sergeant Christopher	professional photographer attached to 2nd Battalion Scots Guards, Western Front
Saunders, Major P. C.	Supply and Transport Corps, siege of Kut
Spooner, Reverend Harold	Church of England padre, siege of Kut
Turner, Private Robert	London Rifle Brigade, Christmas Truce, 1914
Woods, Private H. V.	4th Field Ambulance, Anzac, Gallipoli

BIBLIOGRAPHY

(Place of publication is London unless otherwise shown.)

The main primary source is obviously the photographs themselves and their supporting documentation of accession registers and catalogues held by the Department of Photographs at the Imperial War Museum. In addition the Department also holds some of the surviving papers of the Ministry of Information dealing with the administration of official photography. Further material on the general organization of propaganda is available at the Public Record Office scattered through the records of the state departments concerned. Unfortunately the main bulk of the papers of the Ministry of Information seems to have been destroyed not long after it was dismantled; what survives can be found in class INF 4 of the Central Office of Information papers. My main sources for the manner in which the photographs were published in the contemporary illustrated press are the *Daily Mirror*, *The Illustrated London News*, *The Sphere* and *The War Illustrated*.

Adam-Smith, Janet, *John Buchan*, Rupert Hart Davis, 1965.
Badsey, S. D., 'British official photography in the First World War', Imperial War
    Museum unpublished monograph, 1981.
Baldwin, Herbert, *A War Photographer in Thrace*, T. Fisher Unwin, 1933.
Barker, A. J., *The Neglected War, Mesopotamia 1914–18*, Faber & Faber, 1967.
Bean, C. E. W., and Gullett, H. S., *Official History of Australia in the War, Vol. XII,
    Photographic Record of the War*, Sydney, Angus & Robertson, 1939.
Beaverbrook, Lord, *Men and Power 1917–18*, Hutchinson, 1956.
Bickel, Lennard, *In Search of Frank Hurley*, Sydney, Macmillan of Australia, 1980.
Brownrigg, Rear-Admiral Sir Douglas, *Indiscretions of the Naval Censor*, Cassell & Co.,
    1920.
Buchan, John, *Memory-Hold-The-Door*, Hodder & Stoughton, 1920.
Canadian War Record Office Reports 1917 and 1918.
Carmichael, Jane, 'Photographers at Passchendaele', *Imperial War Museum Review*
    no. 2, 1987.
    'Home Front 1914–18: Photographs of G. P. Lewis and Horace Nicholls', *Creative
    Camera* no. 247/8, July/August 1985.
Carver, Field Marshal Lord, *The Seven Ages of the British Army*, Weidenfeld & Nicolson,
    1984.
Charteris, Brigadier General Sir John, *At G.H.Q.*, Cassell, 1931.
Coe, Brian, *Cameras*, Marshall Cavendish, 1978.
Cook, Sir Edward, *The Press in Wartime*, Macmillan, 1920.
Driberg, Tom, *Swaff*, Macdonald and Jane's, 1974.
Falls, Cyril, *The Great War*, New York, G. P. Putnam's, 1959.
Fralin, Francis, *The Indelible Image, Photographs of War*, Exhibition Catalogue Corcoran
    Gallery of Art, Washington DC, published by Henry N. Abrams, New York,
    1985.
Gernsheim, Helmut, *A Concise History of Photography*, Dover, 1986.
Gidal, Tim, *Modern Photojournalism 1910–33*, New York, Collier, Macmillan, 1972.

Hannavy, John, *Roger Fenton of Crimble Hall*, Gordon Fraser, 1975.

Haste, Cate, *Keep the Home Fires Burning*, Allen Lane, 1977.

Hiley, Nicholas, 'Making war: British news media and government control 1914–16', doctoral thesis deposited with Imperial War Museum 1985.

Knightley, Philip, *The First Casualty*, Harcourt Brace Jovanovich, Harvest edition, 1976.

Lewinski, Jorge, *The Camera at War, War Photography from 1848 to the Present Day*, W. H. Allen, 1978.

Liddell Hart's History of the First World War, Pan edition, 1972.

Lytton, Neville, *The Press and the General Staff*, W. Collins, 1921.

McCarthy, Dudley, *Gallipoli to the Somme, The Story of C. E. W. Bean*, Secker & Warburg, 1983.

Marwick, Arthur, *The Deluge, British Society and the First World War*, Bodley Head, 1965.

Women at War, Fontana, 1977.

Masterman, Lucy, *C. F. G. Masterman*, Nicholson & Watson, 1939.

Newhall, Beaumont, *The History of Photography*, Secker & Warburg, 1982.

Reeves, Nicholas, *Official British Film Propaganda during the First World War*, Croom Helm, 1982.

Robinson, Peter, 'Canadian photojournalism during the First World War', *History of Photography*, vol. 2, no. 1, 1978.

Sanders, Michael, and Taylor, Philip, *British Propaganda during the First World War*, Macmillan, 1982.

Tausk, Peter, *Photography in the 20th Century*, Focal Press, 1980.

Thomas, Lowell, *Sir Hubert Wilkins*, New York, Arthur Barker, 1961/62.

T'Serclaes, Baroness de, and Chisholm, Mairi, *The Cellar House of Pervyse*, A. C. Black, 1917.

Ward, John, *A Short History of the Camera*, Fountain Press, 1984.

Wellington House Report 1916, 'Third report on the work conducted for the Government at Wellington House'.

Yardley, Michael, *Backing into the Limelight, A Biography of T. E. Lawrence*, Harrap, 1985.

INDEX

References to photographs are in italics.

Acland, W.D. *106–7*, 110
Admiralty 48
Admiralty Shipyard Labour Department *109*, 114
Africa 76
Aitken, M. (Lord Beaverbrook) 17, *18*, 20, 48, 52, 55, 56, 110, 148
Aitken, T. 65, 66, 67, *70*
Aleppo 82
Allenby, Sir E. 79, 82, 83
America 16, 17, 60, 67, 81, 126
Armistice 47, 144
Army of Occupation (1918) 71
Ashurst, G. 52
Asquith, H. H. 17
HMS *Audacious* 118
Australia 20–1, 126; at Gallipoli 35, 37–8, 49, 53; numbers of photographs 142; official photographers 60; photographic record 20–1, 56, 74, 149, 150–1; *see also* Bean, C.
Australia and New Zealand Army Corps (ANZAC) 35, 37, 39, 76, 124
Australian photographs, *8, 12–13, 22–3, 43, 45, 58–9, 61, 62, 63*
Australian War Memorial Collection 38
Australian War Museum 150
Australian War Records Office 21, 56, 85
Auto Graflex (camera) 9

Baghdad 86, 90, 94, 96
Baldwin, H. *8*, 49, 56, *57–8*
Barrett, Sir A. 86
Bartholomew, H. G. 66, 144
Basra 88
Bean, C. 20, 37, 38, *43*, 44, 48, 56, 60, 65, 74, 149
Beatty, Sir D. 111, 118
Beaverbrook, Lord *see* Aitken, M.

Beirut 82
Belgium 25, 47
Bell Syer, L. S. 88
Belsen *147*
Black Sea 35
Boer War 131
Borden, Sir R. 17
Brady, M. vii
British Expeditionary Force 25
British official photographs *7, 15, 18, 19, 33, 37, 38, 39, 40–1, 46–7, 51, 64, 65, 66, 67, 68, 69, 70, 71, 72, 73, 83, 84, 85, 92, 93, 94, 95, 99, 105, 108, 109, 112–13, 115, 120, 131–2, 134, 135, 141, 146, 149, 152–3*
British Red Cross Society photograph, *136–7*
Broodseinde, battle of 63, 68
Brooks, E. *7, 33, 37, 38, 39, 40–1, 51, 65, 66, 68, 105, 146*; appointment 3, 4, 16; cameras 9; and E. Knocker and M. Chisholm 34; Gallipoli *36–7, 39*, 110; and Naval record 99, 111; official photographer on Western Front 48–9, 52–3, 60–1, 63, 66; record of 142; stature of 144
Brown, C. 111
Brownrigg, Sir D. (Chief Naval Censor) 36, 37, 98, 110, 111, 118
Buchan, J. 17, 20, 21, 65, 81
Burgess, J. W., *100*
Byrne, S. C. 78, *78, 79*

cameras: Auto Graflex 9; of First World War 7–11; Folding Pocket Kodak 10; Goerz Anschutz *7, 8*, hand held 6; Houghton Sanderson 9; Kodak Autographic Special 11, *14*; Kodak Panoram 9; Leica 145; Mackenzie Wishart envelopes 9; in nineteenth century 3; soldiers' 11, *14*; Vest Pocket Kodak 10

163